Executing Strategy for
Business Results

The Results-Driven Manager Series

The Results-Driven Manager series collects timely articles from *Harvard Management Update, Harvard Management Communication Letter,* and the *Balanced Scorecard Report* to help senior to middle managers sharpen their skills, increase their effectiveness, and gain a competitive edge. Presented in a concise, accessible format to save managers valuable time, these books offer authoritative insights and techniques for improving job performance and achieving immediate results.

Other books in the series:

A Timesaving Guide

THE RESULTS-DRIVEN MANAGER

Executing Strategy for Business Results

· · ·

Harvard Business School Press

Boston, Massachusetts

Library of Congress Cataloging-in-Publication Data

Executing strategy for business results.
        p.   cm. — (The results-driven manager series)
    ISBN-13: 978-1-4221-1464-3 (pbk. : alk. paper)
    ISBN-10: 1-4221-1464-3
  1. Strategic planning.
    HD30.28.E956 2007
    658.4'021—dc22   2007000882

Contents

Contents

Strategies for Growing Your Company

Contents

Strategies for Surmounting Special Challenges

Introduction

• • •

We live in a time of accelerating change in the business landscape. Technological advances, shifts in customer preferences, regulatory changes, globalization, new competitors—these and other complex forces are buffeting organizations like never before. To survive *and* thrive under these conditions, companies must constantly formulate effective strategies– their plans for differentiating themselves from competitors. And they must execute those strategies flawlessly.

Defining and carrying out a competitive strategy requires tight coordination among managers and employees at every level in your organization. Everyone must not only understand the strategic direction the company is aiming for; they must also ensure that their everyday efforts support that strategy. When top management, you, your peers, and employees are all pulling in the same direction, you generate valuable business results:

- You help your company grow and stay ahead of rivals.

- You identify and seize advantage of profitable new opportunities—for example, serving new markets through innovative products and services, or achieving unprecedented efficiency in your operations.

- You make smarter decisions about how to invest your time, energy, and budgetary dollars by channeling those resources only into initiatives that support your company's strategy.

- You surmount daunting business challenges more deftly—such as helping your organization succeed during an economic downturn or running your unit or department at top performance even if you're short-staffed.

As appealing as these advantages are, planning and executing strategy isn't easy. Indeed, many strategic initiatives never get off the ground. Why? During the planning stage alone, you face numerous difficult decisions—and you risk making a serious misstep at each one. For example, you have to figure out which of the many new developments you see happening in the business have important ramifications for your company. Does a change in consumer tastes, for instance, constitute a threat to your current offerings—or an opportunity to serve an entirely new market profitably? How will you avoid the all-too-common cognitive biases that can lead to inadvisable strategies—such as assuming that customers will want the new product you're designing or that a strategy which worked in the past will work just as well now?

Also, how far out should you look as you craft a competitive strategy—three years? Five? Fifteen? And of the many possible strategic scenarios you believe could emerge on the business horizon, how do you determine which of them is *most* likely to take shape—and when? Moreover, at any point in time, the changes unfolding in the business arena represent a wide variety of alluring opportunities. How should you decide which of them to pursue? Of the changes that pose threats, how will you determine which of them is the most serious?

Clearly, strategic planning is rife with questions and potential pitfalls. But even if you resolve those questions and sidestep the pitfalls, your well-informed and brilliantly crafted strategy will prove useless unless you can execute it skillfully. To put your strategy into action, you must master a broad range of skills.

For example, you need to align your unit behind the corporate strategy. Alignment means identifying the specific unit-level actions, performance, and projects that will best support the high-level strategy that your company has defined. If you lead the marketing team for example, which marketing strategies will most help your company achieve its strategic goal of carving out new markets or winning a reputation as a cost leader in its industry? If you head a customer call center, how might you redesign key processes to support your organization's objective of increasing customer loyalty and profitability?

Even after you've achieved this alignment, you'll need to maintain it when circumstances shift yet again. For example, what will you do if you lose several crucial, talented employees to rival firms? When the technology you're using becomes obsolete? When an unforeseen competitor suddenly looms on the horizon and changes all the rules of the game? Maintaining alignment in the face of continual change requires strategic flexibility—another essential skill.

Thankfully, mastering the skills needed to define and carry out strategy *is* possible. And this volume will help you. You'll find one section devoted entirely to tactics for planning your strategy. Another concentrates on strengthening your strategic skills—including creating and maintaining strategic alignment, managing the risks involved in selecting and following a strategic direction, and remaining flexible in your strategies. An additional section focuses on strategies for growing your company, since profitable growth plays a central role in any organization's health and competitive positioning. The final section explores a set of special strategic challenges you might expect to encounter—surviving an economic downturn, running your department when you're understaffed, getting competitive advantage from outsourcing—and lays out suggestions for tackling those challenges.

Here's a closer look at what you'll find in this volume:

Planning Your Strategy

Many managers find strategic planning challenging. The articles in this section introduce common planning pitfalls and provide guidelines for circumventing them. In "Strategic Planning—Why It's Not Just for Senior Managers Anymore," business writer Marie Gendron starts things off by making a compelling business case for what she calls "expanded strategic planning." Companies that use expanded strategic planning involve a broad range of managers and employees in development of strategy—and get remarkable results.

For example, Electronic Data Systems gathered input from a major cross-section of employees on where the company stood in its markets, what its current strengths and weaknesses were, and where its future opportunities lay. It then used that input to map out a three-year strategic plan. The approach paid big dividends—in the form of significant market expansion and a jump in revenues. Gendron provides tips for designing an expanded strategic planning process—including ensuring that everyone knows how the company is doing financially and arming all workers with the strategic information they need to do their jobs in a way that furthers the company's market goals.

In "Cognitive Bias in Everyday Strategic Planning," business writer Loren Gary introduces several common mental barriers that can stymie managers during the strategic planning process, and explains how to avoid them. For example, one cognitive bias causes managers to seek only information confirming their assumption that a particular product or service will appeal to consumers. To counteract this bias, you need to systematically take the opposite perspective—putting yourself in customers' shoes and asking, "Why might this product fail?"

Another bias causes managers to assume that a strategic alliance that worked for one project (such as a co-marketing agreement with another company) should be repeated for other projects. To combat this bias, broaden your information base by involving in the decision-making session more people than would typically participate. Challenge participants to present disconfirming evidence for why repeating a strategic alliance may *not* be wise for a new project—no matter how successful it was on a previous effort.

The next article, "Scenario Planning Reconsidered," introduces scenario planning as a strategy formulation tool and explains how to get the most from it. Through scenario planning, managers use their intuition and imagination to craft stories about how their industry might evolve in the future. They then design a strategy for responding to each scenario, should it actually arise. How to use scenario planning? Start by asking people for their views about future developments. Then gather and analyze data on the various trends that affect your business. Sketch out scenarios—"what if" stories depicting how your industry's most influential forces might play out. Assess the implications of each scenario for your unit or company and develop signposts for each— events that could indicate that a particular scenario has begun to materialize. Finally, reassess your vision in light of the scenarios, asking yourself whether the vision requires any changes.

The last article in this section is "How to Evaluate Opportunities Quickly and Strategically," by business editor Kirsten D. Sandberg. As Sandberg points out, changes in the business world can create such a large sea of possibilities that can capsize a company while it's trying to decide which ones to pursue. To avoid this outcome, establish "simple rules" for identifying the few opportunities you want to explore among the many possibilities out there.

For instance, "boundary rules" enable you to distinguish opportunities that align with your company's core ideology from those that don't. American Express, for example, forges strategic partnerships with only those firms that can deliver unique benefits—not simply "me too" results—to Amex's customers. Amex also insists on priority access to the partner's resources and information. Moreover, partners must have the infrastructure needed to meet Amex's service requirements. "Exit rules" are also useful: they help you determine when to "cut bait." To illustrate, Amex establishes performance objectives for each of its strategic partners and ties its exit strategy to those objectives.

Strengthening Your Strategic Skills

To implement a well-planned strategy, you need a set of strategic skills. The articles in this section lay out those skills and offer suggestions for strengthening them. Business editor Paul Michelman begins the section by introducing the first of three articles on strategic alignment. In "How Will You Better Align with Strategy?" he defines the three steps necessary to align your unit behind your company's strategy: (1) Make sure you have a clear understanding of the strategy, (2) Turn that strategy into something actionable for your staff, and (3) Implement procedures that will keep your unit aligned with the strategy despite shifting conditions.

Michelman then provides recommendations for handling step 1 if your company hasn't explicitly defined the high-level strategy. For example, "Begin by asking. Seek your boss's interpretation and, where appropriate, reach even higher. Look not only for face-to-face input; speeches by the CEO, reports to shareholders, and other documents can reveal valuable insights." Then "compare what you hear and read about strategic priorities with where the company's resources are going. There may be a lot of talk about innovation, but if the biggest portions of the expenditure pie are earmarked for marketing the existing product line, that says something quite different."

In "How Will You Turn Top-Level Strategy into Unit-Level Action?" Michelman turns to step 2 of the strategic alignment process. To convert corporate strategy into an actionable agenda for your unit, communicate the strategy to your employees using relevant context and language. Involve your team in defining how the strategy relates to your unit and what alignment will require. Then ensure that each direct report is on board—and on track. By directly involving your employees in discussions on how to execute strategy in your unit, you can greatly enhance their commitment to the strategy and to their individual roles in carrying it out.

Michelman's "How Will You Maintain Alignment?" explores step 3 of the alignment process by providing suggestions for keeping "everyone's eyes on the strategic prize" despite shifting circumstances. One idea is to "connect each project to strategy" by ensuring that projects are completed on time and within budget and that they advance the company as far as possible toward its strategic objectives. Also, "measure and reward" strategic performance by custom-building metric and reward systems to support the strategy. For example, tie a portion of your team's total compensation to its results as they relate to top-line strategy.

Finally, "wage war on short-term thinking." Help employees shift their attention from scoring short-term gains (such as exceeding this month's revenue targets) to ensuring long-term focus on the strategy. You can encourage long-term focus by giving each employee a document with the annual corporate objectives listed on the top—and asking each to write down five to six initiatives he or she needs to accomplish during the year to help the company meet its goals.

In addition to alignment, strategic skills include managing the risk involved in setting and implementing strategy. Loren Gary's article "The Right Kind of Failure" addresses this issue of risk. Whether your strategy involves innovating radical new products or services, defining new markets, or overhauling your business model, it will have inherent risks. For example, perhaps an initiative designed to support the strategy will fail, experience delays, or cost much more than you expected. Or maybe competitive forces will take a turn you didn't anticipate—rendering your new strategy useless.

Though risk is inherent in any strategy, avoidance of risk at all costs won't help your company. To enable managers and employees to define and carry out strategy despite the risks, you need to create a safe environment for experimenting and for learning from mistakes. Guidelines include initiating experiments (such as prototypes for new products) with assumptions about what you might learn, assessing initiatives' outcomes as quickly as possible, and experimenting on a small scale, so that any failure will have relatively minor ramifications.

In "Five Steps to Thriving in Times of Uncertainty," business writer Peter Jacobs focuses on flexibility, another important strategic skill. To maintain strategic flexibility—the ability to confront change and uncertainty by adjusting your strategy—Jacobs offers several suggestions. For example, view strategic decisions as a portfolio of options. "Organizations usually have multiple projects and initiatives under way simultaneously," he writes, "and it's critical that leaders not let one or two dominate their attention. As markets shift, seemingly less significant initiatives may quickly become the most valuable." Also, continually gather fresh perspectives on the strategic situation, for instance, by routinely rotating managers through different roles so they can get the "big picture" of how your company operates. And partner with other firms to mutually capitalize on complementary resources and gain fresh ideas and insights on what's happening in your industry.

Management consultant John Hagel III provides additional thoughts about strategic flexibility in his article "Web Services: Technology as a Catalyst for Strategic Thinking." According to Hagel, Web services—technologies that automate connections across applications and data—can enhance flexibility and collaboration within an organization. With greater flexibility and collaboration, you reduce inefficiency and mobilize more resources to deliver greater value to customers. For example, Dell Computer uses Web services to connect with suppliers and third-party logistics providers in ways that enable Dell to assemble computers to order with unusual speed—a competency essential to its strategy and business model.

Strategies for Growing Your Company

Many corporate strategies have growth—in sales, revenues, profitability, market share, and other dimensions—as their ultimate objective. For that reason, the articles in this section focus on strategies for spurring and maintaining growth. Business writer Theodore Kinni opens the section with his article "How Strategic Is Your Sales Strategy?" which explores the tactics that high-performing companies use to enhance sales by infusing their sales forces with a more vigorous sense of strategy.

Kinni presents several practices for enhancing sales. For example, "put the right people in the right seats"— that is, hire the right people into your sales organization. CIBA Vision developed a profiling instrument that attempts to match the personality traits of prospective account executives with those found in the company's top-performing sales people. The resulting profile then became the basis of a tool the firm uses when hiring. Seeking specific traits in new hires gives CIBA Vision the type of people it needs to be successful.

Business writer Adrian Mello stays with the theme of growth in "Creative Destruction or Concentrating on the Core: Which Is the Right Path to Growth?" As the rate of change has accelerated dramatically, Mello writes, companies must continually reinvent themselves—sometimes even exiting successful businesses in order to move into more profitable ones. That is, constantly focusing on your core business may not always be sufficient to ensure sustainable growth.

Yet your core business can help you fuel new growth by enabling you to expand into "profitable adjacencies" (businesses that are closely related to your core). While evaluating adjacencies, make sure you have a clearly defined core. Then look for the opportunities nearby with the most potent sources of competitive differentiation and advantage—for example, new products, new channels, new customer segments, new geographies, new value chain steps, new technologies, and new businesses. For instance, if you're in retail, consider businesses that share customer bases of manufacturing processes with your core.

This section concludes with "The Latest Thinking on Growth," which distills advice from three books on the subject: Robert Tomasko's *Go for Growth!*, Richard Whiteley and Diane Hessan's *Customer Centered Growth*, and Dwight Gertz and João P. A. Baptista's *Grow to Be Great*. By sifting through these books, you can find numerous generic strategies for stimulating growth. One strategy is to grow by selling ever more to the same base of carefully selected customers—those representing the lion's share of your profits. For example, USAA initially sold auto insurance to military officers and then began providing them with a full portfolio of financial services—to the tune of $6 billion a year. Another growth strategy entails rethinking how you get your product or service to customers. To illustrate, by selling home improvement materials direct to consumers through its stores, The Home Depot became the distribution channel for its industry—and sucked up much of the profit that used to go to manufacturers or less efficient middlemen.

Strategies for Surmounting Special Challenges

In addition to the need to enhance growth, your unit or company may face other challenges that require savvy strategies. The articles in this section explore three such challenges and provide suggestions for crafting strategies that will help you overcome each.

In "Taking Advantage of a Downturn," Bain consultants Sarabjit Singh Baveja, Steve Ellis, and Darrell K. Rigby maintain that a recession, though painful, can actually present valuable opportunities for companies. By defining the right strategy, you can seize advantage of an economic downturn—and score impressive profits. For example, "In 2001, Dell Computer grew unit sales by 11% even as industry sales declined 12%. Realizing that price elasticity sometimes increases during a recession, Dell used sensible price cuts to gain more than six points in U.S. market share and, in the toughest period of all—the fourth quarter of 2001—to capture more than 90% of the profits in its industry."

How to pursue a thoughtful and balanced recession strategy? Identify your key strengths and weaknesses, and use them to measure new strategic options. Also maintain strategic discipline: if the data says your core business is weak, don't try to invest during the downturn until you've fixed the problem. In addition, correct any wrong turns promptly, reevaluating your strategy if it isn't showing results.

In "Strategies for the Shorthanded," Paul Michelman turns to a strategic challenge that's far closer to home: maintaining your unit's performance even if the unit finds itself on the wrong end of a workforce reduction. Under these tough circumstances, staying focused is a must. Examine each of your goals, and ask questions such as "Is this goal aligned with the company's strategy?" "How will it satisfy stakeholders?" and "Does my unit have the resources to achieve this goal?" Also, "remember the little picture." Use small successes as a motivational tool, and make sure everyone in your unit understands the long-term strategy. Set weekly and even daily priorities to ensure that short-term achievements support longer-term goals.

The final article in this section is "How to Think Strategically About Outsourcing," by business writer Martha Craumer. This selection addresses the challenges posed by companies' increasing interest in outsourcing not only everyday business processes (such as payroll and IT) but strategically significant functions (such as manufacturing and logistics). Yet despite outsourcing's promise, only 54% of companies are satisfied with it, down from more than 80% fifteen years ago.

How to get more from outsourcing? Use it as a tool to drive strategic value, transform businesses, and even reshape industry dynamics. For example, Fender Guitar extracted valuable services from UPS Supply Chain Solutions (SCS). SCS helped Fender rethink its decentralized, country-by-country distribution model in Europe by drawing on best practices from the high-tech industry. Now, instead of keeping stacks of inventory in each country, Fender uses a centralized, pan-European system that cuts inventory, warehousing, and transportation costs.

As you read the selections in this volume, consider how you might start applying the insights and practices offered by the article authors. For example:

- How do you and other managers in your organization currently plan strategy? What changes, if any, would help you improve the planning process? For example, could you find more effective ways to avoid the cognitive biases that typically stymie strategic planners? Could you create some "simple rules" for distinguishing the most promising strategic opportunities from the merely possible?

- Which of your strategic skills—including alignment, risk management, strategic flexibility—could most benefit from strengthening? And how might you enhance those skills? For instance, could you tighten the alignment between your unit and the high-level corporate strategy by gathering more input from employees on how their daily work can help support the company's strategy?

- What strategies is your company currently using to spur growth—whether it's in sales, revenues, profit margin, market share, or some other measure? How might you make those strategies more effective? For example, could your company make better use of its core competencies to expand into adjacent businesses?

- Is your unit or company currently operating during an economic downturn? Is the organization understaffed? Has the company decided to step up its use of outsourcing to gain strategic advantages? How might you apply the ideas in this volume to surmounting one or more of these three special challenges?

Planning Your Strategy

• • •

Many managers find strategic planning challenging.
The articles in this section introduce common planning
pitfalls and provide guidelines for circumventing them.
In the pages that follow, you'll find suggestions for
involving other managers and employees in developing
strategy, as well as avoiding common mental barriers
that can stymie managers during the strategic planning
process. Additional selections provide guidelines for
using scenario planning as a strategy formulation tool
and for identifying the strategic opportunities you want
to explore among the many possibilities that may be
unfolding in your industry.

Strategic Planning—Why It's Not Just for Senior Managers Anymore

· · ·

Marie Gendron

When Electronic Data Systems Corp. (EDS) decided to take a new look at its business strategy a while back, it took great pains to get ideas from more than just its top executives. In fact, 2,500 of the company's 55,000 employees eventually participated. The two-step strategic planning process began with forums and meetings designed to get input from workers at all levels and in all departments about exactly where the company stood in its markets, what its current strengths and weaknesses were, and where its future opportunities lay. Using the information gleaned from this first phase, EDS's CEO and a team of senior executives mapped out a three-year strategic plan designed to achieve the goals set by the larger group.

The exercise resulted in a significant market expansion for EDS, which had traditionally relied on business services—for example, creating tools to convert computer platforms from one operating system to another—for the bulk of its revenue. Now, the company is aggressively pursuing clients interested in redoing their business processes and in electronic commerce—Web-site creation and hosting services to help customers make sense of the Internet. This new approach is already paying real dividends: EDS recorded $16.3 billion in total revenue for 1997, a company record and nearly double the previous year's total. "I attribute a lot of that to focus, which is what strategy brings you," says John Harris, vice president for marketing and a leader of EDS's strategic planning effort. "The thing we're trying to enforce is that developing strategy is the responsibility of everybody in the company."

EDS isn't the only company that has taken strategic decision making out of the boardroom. A growing number of companies are realizing that success demands the best market information *and* the ability to act on it quickly. A winning formula requires *every* employee to think strategically about how her or his job fits in with the company's goals. Roger Martin, director of the global consulting firm Monitor Co., argues that managers can no longer afford to think of any of their workers as automatons who merely execute tasks handed down from above. *All* workers make key decisions every day about how they do their jobs, and those decisions can affect a company's strategy—for good or for ill.

But companies must recognize this fact before they can take advantage of it. What follows then are insights gleaned from recent literature as well as from people in the trenches about why an expanded strategic planning process makes sense—and how to operate one in your company.

Opening up the process improves customer relationships and saves time.

"In a wide variety of industries, there's an increasing focus on understanding what the customer wants," notes Shannon Rye Wall of Manus, a strategy consulting firm. "The real difference today is being able to give people what they're looking for. The top managers can get fairly isolated up there in the executive dining room. If you include others [in the strategic planning], you're more likely to get strategies that fit what's going on out there in the marketplace."

"The only way out of the box is to think about a corporation as a 'choice factory,'" continues Martin. "Everybody really is a choice-making entity. There is no bright line you can draw between those who formulate and those who implement."

One vital element in getting employees involved in strategic planning, write Steven L. Goldman, Roger N. Nagel, and Kenneth Preiss in *Agile Competitors and Virtual Organizations,* is to make sure everyone knows how the company is doing financially. The authors cite the examples of Nucor Steel, John Deere's seeder plant, and TRW's remote keyless entry system plant—all of which have successful programs that tie a percentage of employees' income to performance. Moreover, all three companies have taken pay-for-performance a step further by sharing an unprecedented amount of information with the troops. This includes providing short courses for everyone on reading a profit-and-loss statement; releasing timely, detailed, and accurate reports on the company's production and service costs and sales, marketing, and distribution operations; and showing how company figures compare to competitors' costs and sales.

Moreover, including more employees in the planning process spares your company the time and effort needed to get everyone to buy into a strategy that's already been cast in stone. "Most middle managers are not involved in the strategy formation in a meaningful and helpful way," says Martin. "I'm not seeing a whole lot of evidence of a productive solution taking place. What you've had grow up is a whole field of change management, where the focus is how do you get 'buy-in' to strategic choices that have been made at the upper level. How do you build a consensus after the fact? I don't think that's the right answer." At EDS, corporate strategy is constantly adjusted based on feedback from employees. The company has even implemented a formal program called the Value Creation Team, which provides a venue for any employee to come forward with suggestions about new business improvements, or ways to respond better to market demands.

Empowerment should not come at the expense of expertise.

The idea that every worker should be involved in formulating the company's strategic plan does not mean that committees of the most junior people should be charged with deciding what markets to enter or which plants to close. "It's a very flawed notion of empowerment which involves giving people power to make a decision on something they know very little about," cautions Martin. Rather, the idea is to arm all workers with the strategic information they need to do their own jobs in a way that furthers the company's market goals.

Martin argues for the concept of a cascade of choices flowing down through the organization. The CEO and top lieutenants develop an overall corporate strategy, which is then explained to the rest of the management team. The managers make choices about their departments' marketing plans, sales goals, staffing needs, and so on, based on the corporate strategy, and disseminate their decisions to their teams, explaining what they hope to accomplish and what they expect of the subordinates. The workers then make their own choices about how to do their jobs based on that information.

The cascade of information should not just flow downward.

Workers who are informed about where the company is headed and how it plans to get there can supply their managers with invaluable front line information that can often improve the company's overall strategy. Martin cites the example of a garbage truck driver for a large waste management company that was trying to improve the efficiency of a new processing plant. The driver's manager described how the new processing facility worked, explaining that it processed two distinct types of waste that had to be separated from each other. The manager then asked the driver to think about his daily route in the context of how the company had set up the new facility. The driver proposed reorganizing his route to include 10 locations that had predominantly one kind of waste in the morning and the other 10, which had predominantly the second kind of waste, in the afternoon. The result was a significant saving of money and sorting time.

"There's so much data that's in the head of that garbage truck driver," Martin points out. "The only way you can access that is to turn him into a choice maker and give him the context of the choices that were made at least one level up the chain. Once you get this cascade going, there will be this flow of information. People care about the context of choices once they've gotten some of its fruits."

Middle managers become strategy ambassadors.

Stephen Wall, president of Manus, believes middle managers can play key roles in an enlarged strategic planning process, disseminating information about corporate strategy to the lower ranks and bringing front line knowledge back to the top executives. Vinyl resin manufacturer Geon Co., says Wall, has had great success utilizing middle managers this way. Senior management, together with 80 people from Geon's operations group, worked to create a new strategic vision. The company then developed a process by which middle managers could talk to every one of the 1,700 employees, helping each employee link the new vision to his or her own job. At the end of those sessions, employees were asked to fill out an anonymous response form. Some 95% of the respondents said they were fully committed to achieving the vision; 87% said they would make changes in the way they did their work based on what they learned in the sessions.

When your formal authority excludes you from strategic planning, create the cascade yourself.

What if you're a manager at a company that still relies solely on top executives to create strategy and everyone else to merely implement the top brass's decisions? Don't despair, experts say: you can still help shape your company's strategic plan. "You're not limited in any organization by the constraints of your formal role in the organizational chart," says Stephen Wall. "In any business, your ability to marshal a logical argument and present it in an inspiring way is one of the most powerful tools you have as a manager. Even the most Draconian organizations will listen to a good idea."

Middle managers are often the ones who first recognize when a company's business strategy is no longer in tune with the marketplace. In a 1996 *Harvard Business Review* article entitled "Strategy as Revolution," Gary Hamel describes a situation in which a group of middle managers became "strategy activists" because they were concerned that their company was foundering in the marketplace and was in danger of forfeiting the future to its competitors.

The managers, none of whom were corporate officers, formed what they called a "delta team" and began working quietly behind the scenes—without senior management's permission or knowledge—to convince their peers that it was time to rethink the company's basic strategic beliefs. After several months, their conviction took root among a cross-section of managers, who started asking senior executives difficult questions about whether the company was in control of its destiny and whether it was ahead of or behind the industry's change curve. Senior management ultimately conceded it could

> "There's so much data that's in the head of that garbage truck driver . . . The only way you can access that is to turn him into a choice maker."

not answer the tough questions and began a comprehensive effort—including hundreds of employees—to reshape the company's strategic vision. The end result: a refocused mission and a doubling of revenues over the next five years.

Instead of being annoyed or threatened by such initiative on the part of middle managers, Shannon Wall says many senior managers would welcome it. "What we hear from senior people most often is, 'Why aren't they [subordinates] coming up with more stuff?'" After all, write the authors of *Agile Competitors*, "The objective is to provide universal ownership of problems that affect the company's bottom line, in particular, to promote universal ownership of customer gratification as everybody's business." Apparently, this objective has become so critical, not even the hoary old mindset that sees strategic planning and implementation as distinct functions will stand in the way.

For Further Reading

Agile Competitors and Virtual Organizations: Strategies for Enriching the Customer by Steven L. Goldman, Roger N. Nagel, and Kenneth Preiss (1997, John Wiley & Sons)

The New Strategists: Creating Leaders at All Levels by Stephen J. Wall and Shannon Rye Wall (1995, The Free Press)

Strategic Pay: Aligning Organizational Strategies and Pay Systems by Edward E. Lawler (1990, Jossey-Bass Publishing)

"Strategy as Revolution" by Gary Hamel (*Harvard Business Review,* July–August 1996)

Reprint U9805A

Cognitive Bias in Everyday Strategic Planning

• • •

Loren Gary

Fast-cycle decision making, as the previous article demonstrates, is about learning to pedal faster, but not exclusively so. It's also about redesigning the derailleur so that your company can make better decisions. The company that focuses obsessively on achieving breakneck speed, neglecting its decision-making processes, is headed for a crash.

An April 1998 *Harvard Management Update* article examining judgment heuristics—simplifying strategies, or decision-making shortcuts—left some readers with the impression that cognitive biases, the faulty patterns of thought resulting in the misapplication of judgment heuristics, are esoteric phenomena managers rarely encounter. Nothing could be further from the truth. Cognitive biases are, in fact, a lot like kudzu: they are introduced for the best of reasons, but then quickly threaten to take over the entire managerial landscape.

Strategic growth initiatives—new-product development, alliances, and mergers and acquisitions—seem especially prone to these unconscious errors in judgment. The bias creeps in unawares, becoming evident only in hindsight, in the light of some disastrous consequence. Three frequently encountered scenarios follow—each one illustrating a different cognitive bias—along with commentary from expert practitioners about how to avoid the decision-making error involved.

New-Product Development and the Confirmation Bias

The confirmation bias results when managers seek confirming evidence for what they think is true, or for the outcome they want to achieve, but neglect the search for disconfirming evidence. This bias comes into play in new-product development, says Richard Gooding, president of Strategic Advantage, Inc., when companies forget to "look at why the customer might not want the product that's being designed." Citing the example of Arizona Instruments, Gooding notes that the board of directors started pressing for a new product line not long after the company went public in 1989. "They came upon a new process for detecting underground gas leaks that was about 100 times more accurate than any existing technology. At the same time, the Environmental Protection Agency was getting legislation through Congress mandating that all underground gasoline storage tanks be continuously tested. So the thinking at Arizona Instruments was that it was going to introduce this superior technology at a time when an enormous demand for it was coming on line.

"The company sold its first installation incorporating the new technology in 1991—and that was the only unit it ever sold. The CEO acknowledged later that Arizona Instruments never put itself in the shoes of one of the intended customers for this technology—a Texaco or Conoco—and asked, 'How badly do we want to detect leaks in our underground gasoline storage tanks?' The answer, of course, was that they didn't want to know very badly at all—they just wanted to stay out of trouble with the Environmental Protection Agency. The technology that Arizona Instruments had developed could detect a leak the size of a glass of water from a 90,000-gallon tank. But EPA regulations allowed tanks of that size to leak 1,500 gallons of gas." In other words, customers didn't need or want so sensitive an instrument—but Arizona Instruments never bothered to ask.

When the federal government passes legislation, it typically leaves enforcement up to the states, which means that implementation occurs slowly. In the case of the EPA legislation concerning underground gas tanks, Gooding recalls, "only 40% of the nation's gas stations were in compliance six to seven years after the legislation passed." Arizona Instruments neglected to study how such legislation gets implemented, so it failed to anticipate why demand for its technology would never come on line. Seduced by the capability of the technology itself, Gooding continues, "management could see only why customers would be so excited to buy it."

The key to counteracting the confirmation bias in new-product development scenarios, says Gooding, who has been helping companies think about strategic growth initiatives for more than eighteen years, is to "systematically get managers to take the opposite perspective. To put themselves in the customer's shoes and ask, 'Why might this product fail?'" Gooding facilitated such a conversation—he describes it as "a structured brainstorming process"—with Arizona Instruments some years later, when the company was planning to introduce a new moisture analyzer onto the market. "There were a number of issues that came up. Some related to reliability, quality, competitive response, equipment maintenance—60 or 70 items in all. But most interesting to me was the comment that it was just plain ugly—when I had the team prioritize the items, this one rose to the top. The team went back and redesigned the product inside and out. And it won an award for one of the 100 best products for 1997."

Strategic Alliances and the Availability Heuristic

Assuming that the most readily available information is the most pertinent information is an example of the availability heuristic. Biases that derive from this heuristic often crop up when companies are considering strategic alliances. A major reason for this, says Quinn Spitzer, chairman and CEO of the management consulting firm Kepner-Tregoe, is that "nobody is sure what strategic alliances are—they can range from a simple, circumscribed comarketing agreement all the way to a sharing of employees. Consequently, a 'collection phenomenon' often results": if one alliance is successful, managers will tend to say, "Let's do 20 more exactly like this one." The error, Spitzer continues, lies in the inference that the structure of the most recent alliance should govern all subsequent alliances—even when the needs of the companies involved are quite different.

The remedy for the availability bias, says Gooding, consists of "counteracting the natural tendency to look for confirming information" by broadening the information base. "The decision about a strategic alliance is often made by a pretty small team—three or four senior managers. I make sure to involve in the decision-making session more people than would typically be involved. The goal is to balance out the information and perspectives that different people have available to them, to bring to bear on the decision information that the senior managers may not have. Having more people present increases the likelihood of uncovering disconfirming information.

"But you can't treat all the perceptions as equals," Gooding emphasizes. "So it's critical to have the team prioritize the various comments. Then not only do you get all these different perspectives brought to bear, but you also get an overall rating of the importance of each particular issue. This ensures that the decision won't be driven just by who recalled what and how important they think it is. It will be driven by all these people recalling a broader set of issues and then systemically rating them based on a group discussion."

Mergers and Acquisitions and the Nonrational Escalation of Commitment

Our responses to decisions are influenced by the way we frame information, observes Max Bazerman in *Judgment in Managerial Decision Making*. But many managerial decisions, he writes, "concern a series of choices rather than an isolated decision. We are prone to a particular type of bias when decisions are approached serially—namely, a tendency to escalate commitment."

Potential mergers and acquisitions are often ripe for just this kind of misjudgment, says Gooding. "Several years ago, the American Management Association did a study of mergers and acquisitions. The biggest surprise, respondents said, was that the process of integrating the accounting systems between the two companies took much longer than expected. Many companies thought it would take six months but it ended up taking two and a half years. Now, if you don't have the comptroller, or the head of the accounting department, on the team that's considering the acquisition, that fact may never come to light until it's too late."

The extensive due diligence required for a merger or acquisition makes many companies reluctant to conclude that they shouldn't proceed with the deal. "There's a phrase called 'deal heat,'" Gooding explains, "which describes the momentum that is created by such a process. It becomes impossible for the organization to turn back, even though they might think it's not the right deal. Things get exacerbated if there is a bidding war: a company gets wrapped up in the auction-like atmosphere and ends up paying too much for the acquisition."

So it's not surprising, adds Spitzer, that "so many mergers end up being failures. Just look at the pharmaceutical industry—in almost every instance, the combined entity has ended up with less market share than the two independent ones." His conclusion? "The due diligence process creates false beliefs. It enables you to be tremendously emotive. You fall in love with a potential acquisition before fully considering the alternatives."

Questioning your basic assumptions. Cultivating richer, more diverse sources of information and opinion.

Resisting the impulse to be swept away by the emotional flood tide of the new product, technology, or acquisition candidate. In all three scenarios, countering the decision-making bias involves raising it to the level of conscious discussion. "You have to take the time to build a conscious decision-making process," says Spitzer. "Generally, people tend to adjust their objectives as the data relevant to the decision starts coming in. What we try to do with clients is to get them to be very intentional about when and why they're changing the substance and relative weights of the criteria they established at the outset."

For Further Reading

Heads You Win: How the Best Companies Think by Quinn Spitzer and Ronald Evans (1997, Simon & Schuster)

Judgment in Managerial Decision Making by Max Bazerman (4th ed., 1998, John Wiley & Sons)

Tying the Corporate Knot: An AMA Research Report on the Effects of Mergers and Acquisitions edited by Don Lee Bohl (1989, American Management Association)

Reprint U9808D

Scenario Planning Reconsidered

. . .

New week, new threat, new opportunity. The future seems to get here a lot faster these days. The number of possible futures seems greater than ever, too.

With managers struggling to figure out which businesses they should be in three months down the road, how could they possibly have time for scenario planning, which asks them to imagine alternative futures that might exist 3, 10, even 25 years from now? Well, they better make time. When things are changing fast, if you wait for a trend to be validated, it's too late—the window of opportunity will have closed or the threat will have already torpedoed your company. Intuition and a sense of urgency become increasingly important as navigational tools. They help give voice to concerns about developments that have yet to appear on the horizon. This is precisely why scenario planning can be so valuable: it's an intuitive means of identifying and reflecting upon uncertainties that companies face.

Scenario planning differs from traditional approaches to strategic development in two ways:

1. IT'S NOT DESIGNED TO PROVIDE AN ACCURATE PREDICTION OF THE FUTURE. Trend analysis and forecasting seek to identify the single most likely contingency and build the one best strategy for dealing with it. By contrast, scenario planning is based on the premise that you cannot control or predict the future. It helps you envision equally plausible ways that the future might unfold and chart appropriate responses to each.

2. IT RELIES MORE ON NARRATIVE THAN ON TABLES AND GRAPHS. To be sure, trend analysis plays a part in scenario planning. But the scenarios themselves are written as stories. Not only do they put the trends in context, the stories also have a psychological impact that analytical tools lack. They enable managers to tap into their powers of intuition and imagination in a way that's not possible with purely rational exercises. Take, for example, a few of the labels the College of Marin in northern California gave the scenarios it developed: "Beggars at the Banquet" (a situation

characterized by low levels of state funding and a buyer's market for higher education) and "Uncle Harry's Will" (high levels of state funding and a buyer's market for education). Such a metaphor-rich approach is more evocative and thus more likely to challenge people's prevailing mental models.

Scenario planning came into prominence in the 1970s, when it was credited with helping Royal Dutch/Shell anticipate a future in which oil producers held the upper hand in the industry. Consequently, Shell was much better positioned to respond to the OPEC embargo than its competitors. Large, stable companies like Shell have tended to use scenario planning to help identify threats. But today, notes Chris Ertel, cohead of practice at Global Business Network, "We're seeing a much more entrepreneurial usage of scenario planning. There's definitely been a shift in recent years away from using it as a contingency-planning device and more as an idea-generation and innovation device. For some fast-growth firms, the problem is too many options, so they use scenario planning as an opportunity-management tool."

How much does it cost? The answer can vary widely, depending on how detailed an analysis you want. A stripped-down version might run $10,000–$20,000 if you hire an outside consultant, says Ertel. A large-scale project could easily be in excess of $1 million. But not every company needs to do the kind of intricate global analysis that Shell conducted thirty years ago. To develop its scenarios about future oil markets, Shell had to consider the fate of the Soviet Union and its impact on the natural gas market. By contrast, according to a 2000 *Wall Street Journal* article, Duke Energy took a more focused approach. The three scenarios it developed varied depending on U.S. economic growth forecasts and how the Internet might affect the balance of power in energy markets.

Regardless of the purpose and scope of the project, here's the work you need to do to build your scenarios:

Ask your company's top decision makers their views about future developments

Some sample questions: Which decisions do you believe will make or break our company in the next few years? When you try to imagine the world several years from now, which trends do you most want to know about? Which potential developments excite you the most?

Gather and analyze trend data

Put together an information-gathering network if you don't already have one, and compile a list of the external forces that seem most likely to have a significant impact.

Where to Look for Trends

Building scenarios that are plausible as well as mind-expanding calls for broad-based research. Peter Schwartz of Global Business Network recommends the following sources and subjects:

- FORCES OR EVENTS THAT ALTER PUBLIC PERCEPTION: Including television, popular music, and the social and intellectual fringes of our culture.
- REMARKABLE PEOPLE: Sometimes this is a specialist with the ability to illuminate issues outside his own area of expertise.
- FILTERS: For example, a publication that "wades into a muck of new ideas and fringe suggestions and reshapes it in a coherent form."
- TRAVEL: "The single best way to immerse yourself in unfamiliarity."
- NETWORKED SENSIBILITIES: Chat rooms, communities of practice.

Sketch out the scenarios

Each scenario is essentially a "what if" story that takes your list of most influential external forces and weaves them into a coherent narrative. Peter Schwartz, cofounder and chairman of Global Business Network, recommends limiting the number of scenarios to three: your worst nightmare, a fundamentally different but better world, and a world that is basically a continuation of the status quo only better. Don't assign a probability to each scenario—the point of the exercise is to develop equally plausible futures.

Kees van der Heijden, one of Global Business Network's cofounders, likens scenario planning to a wind tunnel in which you test a strategy. As he writes in *Scenarios: The Art of Strategic Conversation,* the scenarios provide "the test conditions, representing various business environments in which the strategy has to perform." Even "those that present extreme cases," he writes, "should represent both plausible conditions of the business environment, and those that are suitable and practical as planning assumptions." So, for example, when Texaco created a scenario that included mass-produced hybrid cars with advanced batteries and fuel cells, it created a back story for the scenario—a description of the economic and technological conditions that would have made this mass production possible. Give each scenario a name to make it more vivid and compelling to your company's leadership.

Assess the implications of each scenario

Even if your scenarios touch on global developments, it's important to articulate the local implications—the immediate consequences of your company's decision making.

Develop signposts for each scenario

Identify signs that could indicate that a particular scenario is materializing. Duke Energy developed scores of indicators—including regulatory trends, environmental issues, and competitors' moves—to help managers determine which scenario seemed to be unfolding.

Reassess your company's vision in light of the scenarios

Managers come away from the exercise with a heightened awareness of the often unconscious assumptions about the future that underlie their strategic decisions. The outcome is not an improved ability to predict the future, but improved organizational decision making—a keener eye for spotting decisions that might otherwise have been missed or denied.

Reprint U0605D

How to Evaluate Opportunities Quickly and Strategically

• • •

Kirsten D. Sandberg

The Internet created a tsunami of opportunity that has distracted many companies from their core businesses. Racing to catch the wave, they spun off online units as if the Internet were a business model rather than a new technology. Only after flushing a lot of "dumb money" down the dot-com drain have they come to their senses.

"Just because the Internet changes everything, doesn't mean that everything about business changes," says Paul

Deninger, chairman and CEO of Broadview, a mergers and acquisitions advisor and private equity specialist. Or, as Ken Fox, managing director of Internet Capital Group, a business-to-business e-commerce firm, puts it, a "healthy tension between profitability and growth . . . focuses execution very well." Built-to-last companies sustain growth *and* generate profits. So for high-growth firms like Amazon.com, the task now is to concentrate on the fiscal fundamentals that generate profits while continuing to grow. Established firms like American Express must learn how to leverage core assets to keep the corporate coffers afloat.

The complicating factor, however, is not a dearth of opportunity but a deluge of it. Opportunity no longer knocks, says Harvard Business School assistant professor Don Sull—it flows like an open fire hydrant. The possibilities can be disorienting: *Should we exploit existing resources or create new ones, fortify our current position or enter new markets? Should we go it alone or find partners?*

Look for Rapids and Dams

With "water, water everywhere," how do managers choose the drop worth drinking? Pick "a small number of strategically significant processes [that] place the company where the flow of opportunities is swiftest and deepest," advises Sull in a recent *Harvard Business Review* article he coauthored with Kathleen Eisenhardt.

Executives like Yahoo! chairman Tim Koogle know that the richest opportunities surface quickly—and unexpectedly—during market chaos. In Yahoo!'s market, chaos exists in the production and distribution of content; Koogle predicts that the best prospects for his

> Pay attention to market chaos. Look for bottlenecks in processes, areas where incumbents have overshot customers' needs, and products with too many features.

firm will be found along the content "food chain." His strategy—start with the most primitive link, mutate it, and build out from there—mirrors the company's tagline: "Yahoo! is the only place anyone would have to go to find and get connected to anything or anyone." Thus, Yahoo! first aggregated pages of information with search tools, moved to communications and connecting tools, and then addressed issues of commerce and secure transactions.

"Look for the bottlenecks" in processes—for example, the bandwidth deficit and the antediluvian user interface—to find opportunities for growth, advises Deninger. In addition, suggests Michael Overdorf, CEO of the consulting firm Innosight, look for overserved customers, areas where incumbents have "overshot what the needs of the market are," and product features that exceed their uses.

What Simple Rules Are—And Aren't

Once you've picked your processes, Sull advises, craft a few simple rules to guide your decisions for fast action and follow-through. Such rules provide just enough structure to navigate confidently through fickle and fast-moving markets—but enough flexibility to improvise in stable, well-structured, and glacially paced marketplaces. They bond people to new undertakings because they quickly convey what matters to a company, where the new venture fits into the overall strategy, and how to measure the venture's success. Sull and Eisenhardt identify five general categories of rules:

1. HOW-TO RULES guide the execution of the process. At Yahoo!, every engineer must work on every project, and new products are launched quietly. At Enron, commodity traders must offset each trade with another that hedges Enron's risk.

2. PRIORITY RULES help you allocate resources so everyone knows what to focus on and how much time, talent, and money to devote to the process.

3. TIMING RULES synchronize a team's efforts with the opportunity at hand and with initiatives across the company. Autodesk, a design software firm, shortened its new-product development schedule from 18–24 months to three months so that it could quickly identify and run with winning products.

4. BOUNDARY RULES enable managers to distinguish the opportunities that align with the company's core ideology from those that don't. American Express, for instance, partners only with firms that can deliver unique benefits—not simply "me-too" results—to Amex's customers. Amex also insists upon priority access to the partner's resources and information, and the partner must have the infrastructure to meet Amex's service requirements.

5. EXIT RULES help managers determine when to cut bait. Amex establishes performance objectives for each of its partnerships and investments and ties its exit strategy to those objectives.

Simple rules typically emerge from years of collective experience—the company's as well as the top management team's—and especially from bad experiences, says Sull. Take, for example, the rules that resulted from Yahoo!'s disappointing early partnerships: no exclusive deals and no service fees. To appreciate how such rules

Pick Your Profit Channel

In their classic book *Built to Last*, James Collins and Jerry Porras wrote that the "underlying processes and fundamental dynamics embedded in the organization" drive the success of visionary firms. For example, the late Bill Hewlett, cofounder of Hewlett-Packard, considered the process of engineering to be one of the firm's most important and enduring assets: not only did this process create new value, it was also continually being created anew as the organization learned.

Consider the following list of processes. Which of them could you use to impose structure on chaotic markets or inject some chaos into stable markets? How could you generate power from your opportunity flow? How would current operations change?

- Research & development
- Product innovation
- Production & manufacturing
- Branding
- New-market entry
- Customer experience
- Partnering
- Mergers & acquisitions
- Spinouts
- Risk management
- Hiring & firing talent
- Management development
- Sales & marketing

work, it's important to understand what they are not. For instance, they are not:

- BIG HAIRY AUDACIOUS GOALS (BHAGs), a term coined by James Collins and Jerry Porras. A BHAG gets people's creative and competitive juices going—a classic example is General Electric's drive to be #1 or #2 in every market that it serves. Simple rules, Sull explains, are tools that managers use to meet such visionary goals.

- THE BUSINESS MISSION, which author Gary Hamel describes as the overall objective of the business model. Simple rules represent a shorthand method for determining whether a particular opportunity will help a firm achieve its business mission.

- IMMUTABLE, LIKE A COMPANY'S CORE VALUES AND CORPORATE PURPOSE. Instead, they are adaptive mechanisms that enable companies to respond quickly. By eliminating bureaucracy so that people can work across traditional lines of command, simple rules help firms respond to the exigencies of the moment.

Simple rules essentially function like *judgment heuristics,* decision-making shortcuts that help managers cope with complexity and uncertainty. But as Harvard Business School professor Max Bazerman cautions in *Judg-*

ment in Managerial Decision Making: (1) "as the amount of ignorance increases, individuals become more overconfident in their fallible judgment," (2) the most "experienced decision makers can be very biased," and (3) "while most 'effective decision makers' are effective in a specific domain, experience . . . can be quite dangerous when [applied] to a different context or when the environment changes."

Consequently, managers must make sure that the rules reflect the latest learning and that employees are applying them to the right circumstances. Schedule "routine checkups to evaluate . . . recent important decisions," Bazerman advises. Over time, your simple rules will become more refined, better able to help you capitalize on the swiftly shifting currents of opportunity.

For Further Reading

"Strategy as Simple Rules" by Kathleen M. Eisenhardt and Donald N. Sull (*Harvard Business Review*, January 2001)

Built to Last by James C. Collins and Jerry I. Porras (1997, HarperBusiness)

Leading the Revolution by Gary Hamel (2000, Harvard Business School Press)

Judgment in Managerial Decision Making by Max Bazerman (1998, John Wiley & Sons)

Reprint U0104B

Strengthening Your Strategic Skills

• • •

To implement a well-planned strategy, you need a specific set of skills. The articles in this section lay out those skills and offer suggestions for strengthening them. You'll discover how to align your employees behind the company's strategy, define the actions needed in your unit to support the firm's strategic direction, and maintain alignment even if circumstances change. Additional selections provide ideas for managing the risk involved in setting and implementing strategy, adjusting your strategy if changes in the business landscape warrant more flexibility, and using Web-based technologies to further strengthen your strategic flexibility.

How Will You Better Align with Strategy?

• • •

Paul Michelman

Lining up a complex and, at best, vaguely hierarchical global corporation behind a strategy that is driven by ever-shifting market conditions is challenging. It not only requires a clear vision supported by lucid top-down communication but also the focused participation of people at every level of the firm, especially unit heads. In their hands rests the daunting responsibility of making corporate strategy meaningful and actionable for their teams.

As Bob Moffat, senior vice president of IBM's Integrated Supply Chain division, noted recently, "I think about strategy every minute of the day—making sure I understand our business strategy and how I can enable that strategy." Moffat is referring here to something that goes deeper than just ensuring that his unit is contributing to corporate goals. They're simply the endpoint; the strategy is the course that senior management has set to get there. To be truly aligned, you must use the corporate strategy to determine *how*—through which resources and processes—you can most effectively help the organization reach its goals.

Accomplishing this requires three basic—though not simple—steps:

1. Making sure you have a clear understanding of the strategy.

2. Turning that strategy into something actionable for your staff.

3. Implementing procedures that will keep your unit aligned with the strategy.

In this installment, we discuss Step 1: making sure that you have a clear understanding of the strategy.

There's no doubt that the responsibility for articulating strategy should rest at the top. But flatter organizations and occasionally imperfect corporate communications systems can often stand in the way of the kind of crystal-clear direction required to steer an aligned organization. Thus the wise executive will take the strategy bull by the horns and seek to enhance her knowledge of the corporate mandate.

Key Questions in the Strategic-Alignment Process

In their work on strategy maps, Balanced Scorecard pioneers Robert Kaplan and David Norton identify the following core strategy questions. Do you have a clear sense of the answers for both your company and your unit?

- How will we succeed financially?
- What must we provide to our customers to achieve our financial vision?
- Which processes must we excel at to satisfy our customers and shareholders?
- What must our organization learn and how must it improve to achieve our goals?

Begin by asking up. Seek your boss's interpretation and, where appropriate, reach even higher. Look not only for face-to-face input; speeches by the CEO, reports to shareholders, and other documents can reveal valuable insights. In some companies, notes Babson College management professor Allan Cohen, strategy is explicit, "but in others, it has to be inferred from top management." What is on their minds? Are they talking about getting costs in line? Are they discussing top-line growth, building market share, or expanding product lines?

Next, compare what you hear and read about strategic priorities with where the company's resources are actually going. There may be a lot of talk about innovation, but if the biggest portions of the expenditure pie are earmarked for marketing the existing product line, that says something quite different.

It's the executive's task to take all the information at hand—overt and subtle, spoken and observed—and integrate it. Given the multiple information sources that you're relying on, it's rarely a bad idea to vet your understanding of the strategy with those around you.

Reprint U0407F

How Will You Turn Top-Level Strategy into Unit-Level Action?

• • •

Paul Michelman

A shift in corporate strategy should affect everyone in the company in some form. Near the top of the organizational chart, the impact often is dramatic. But as you go deeper into the organization, just how the new strategy should manifest itself can become unclear.

The responsibility for creating clarity around what the strategy means at the unit, team, and individual levels—and for seeing that the strategy is carried out—is shared by managers throughout the ranks.

To aid in this effort, we surveyed the experts to compile this three-point plan for converting corporate strategy into an actionable agenda:

1. Communicate the strategy to teams and individuals using relevant context and language.

2. Involve teams in defining how the strategy relates to the unit and what alignment will require.

3. Ensure each direct report is on board and on track.

"The biggest obstacle to alignment is lack of understanding," says Mitchell Goozé, a consultant with Customer Manufacturing Group and former president of Teledyne Components, a division of Teledyne. Why is this? Well, simply repeating the corporate strategy is easy enough, but you must bring the strategy to life for your team—and many executives neglect to do this.

"A manager's job should be to take the corporate goals and strategies and redefine them in a way that makes them real for the people in their department," says Kaye Lauritsen, a managing director and strategic planning consultant with RSM McGladrey. "The simpler and more straightforward, the better." For example, if a key part of the strategy is improving the success rate of new products, communicate how that relates to the customer-service unit you run.

Ultimately, it may be more effective at first to speculate on the strategy's effect on your team—rather than dictate it—because you'll want to make sure the team feels like it is shaping its own plan. Directly involving subordinates in discussions on how to execute strategy can greatly improve employees' commitment to the strategy and to their individual roles in carrying it out.

Of course, managers must facilitate and direct this process, guiding employees to answer these questions:

- How should the strategy affect our unit?

- What must we thus accomplish?

- How will we accomplish it?

With answers in hand, teams can then develop a shared language and framework for how to think and talk about alignment, which will, notes a report from Catalyst Consulting Team, enable people to match "their behavior to a set of commonly understood goals and actions." To reinforce this, Lauritsen suggests using charts and other aids to measure progress toward new objectives.

With team guidelines set, managers should turn their attention to working with direct reports. "Management must ensure that every employee understands how he or she brings value to the company," says Steve Waterhouse, author of *The Team Selling Solution,* and "how their actions will move the company forward." Specifically, managers must ensure that they and their direct reports agree on how the new strategy will affect how each employee sets priorities and manages his time.

Adds Lauritsen, "With a little thought and imagination, each job function can be related" to strategy. Be careful not to overload people with too many directives, she warns. "Determine which ones need to take priority and are most closely aligned to the strategy."

One cautionary note: not all managers will find the road to alignment quite this direct. Most notably, changes in strategy can leave managers with the wrong mix of talent. In such cases, managers must quickly move forward to acquire the people they need and then turn their attention to implementation.

Reprint U0408G

How Will You Maintain Alignment?

• • •

Paul Michelman

It's one thing to get your team focused on recasting its efforts at the outset of major change in corporate strategy; it is quite another to keep everyone's eyes on the strategic prize over time. Coming to your aid, we canvassed the experts to offer these best practices in maintaining long-term alignment with strategy.

Connect Each Project to Strategy

At hpshopping.com, a unit of Hewlett-Packard, two project managers—one each from business and technology—work on every new initiative. "We hold them equally responsible for making the project a success," says Nikhil Behl, vice president of strategy and development. To be successful, a project must not only be completed on time and on budget, but it must also advance the company as far as possible toward its goals.

Throughout the planning and implementation process, the project managers present weekly updates. If at any point Behl feels the team's objectives are not in harmony with the firm's, the project is put on hold and its strategy is fine-tuned.

During the recent implementation of a business analytics system for the IT group, Behl abruptly stopped the deployment when he realized that, if integrated differently, the system could benefit all business units, not just the IT group. Although the delay was inconvenient, the result is an enterprise business intelligence system that has enabled hpshopping.com to run more efficiently, he says. More than 70% of hpshopping.com's staff use the tool daily.

Measure and Reward

At the core of well-aligned firms are metric and reward systems custom-built to support the strategy.

"As strategic initiatives are funded, metrics should be defined and then tracked at all relevant levels of the organization," says John Dinning, vice president of strategy and planning for Teradata, a division of NCR. "This enables companies to measure successes against their goals and to drill down into the details of the business where action is required."

The key here is to facilitate strategy-driven decision making, the linchpin to alignment. "Effective decisions should be fact-based, and require broad access to accurate and comprehensive data," Dinning says.

The right reward systems are essential. Marc Lewis, president, North America, of global executive search consultants Morgan Howard Worldwide, advises tying a portion of a team's total compensation to that team's specific results as they relate to top-line strategy. Doing so rewards the team's success in interpreting changes in corporate strategy, its ability to plan around those changes, and how well the plans were carried out.

Wage War on Short-Term Thinking

Few things frustrate managers more than seeing their best-laid strategic plans derailed by the drive for immediate gains. The pursuit of short-term gains is the common cold of strategic alignment efforts; no permanent cure exists, so it keeps creeping back in.

People naturally try to produce tangible results. Many employees assume that pleasing the boss with this month's numbers, or finding a solution to some seemingly pressing concern, is better than working on a task whose benefits won't be realized until later in the year, says Adrian W. Savage, author of *A Spark from Heaven? The Place of Potential in Organizational and Individual Development*.

To give strategic pursuits more day-to-day urgency, Blanchard Schaefer Advertising & Public Relations ties individual goals to strategic objectives. Annually, each employee is given a document with the corporate objectives listed on the top; employees must write down five to six initiatives they feel they need to accomplish during the year to help the company meet its goals. In consultation with managers, each initiative is broken down into 90-day objectives, which are further subdivided into action items.

Managers meet with subordinates weekly to "coach them on their progress," says principal Ken Schaefer. "These are progress checks where we can openly discuss the successes and challenges team members are having in achieving their objectives."

Reprint U0409F

The Right Kind of Failure

• • •

Loren Gary

Calamities that could have been foreseen are a hot topic of current public-policy debates. They also figure prominently in managerial conversations, so much so that the innovate-at-all-costs attitude of the dot-com heyday seems to have vanished. To some extent, that's a good thing, because in the giddiness of the late 1990s many firms seemed to forget the distinction between a well-planned experiment and a roulette wheel.

But now the pendulum may have swung too far the other way. With recession now a fact, many firms have razor-thin margins of error; they simply can't afford costly mistakes. Not only are they squeezing processes and supply chains for every dollar they can, they're also scaling back their R&D budgets and pulling the plug on new ventures.

This risk-avoidance mindset is understandable but, paradoxically, it too carries a risk. Innovation is not a nice-to-have, even in a downturn, says Amy Edmondson, associate professor at Harvard Business School. "It's a necessity—in fact, companies may need it now more than ever." Discourage risk taking altogether, adopt a zero-tolerance policy on failure, and your company's ability to generate great revenue-producing ideas will dry up.

But of course, there are two kinds of failure. You can live with the calculated risks that don't pan out—these are failures from which your company ultimately benefits, whether it's in terms of improving existing products and services or identifying which new lines of business to avoid. You'll never be able to bring breakthrough ideas to market successfully unless your unit or company culture is able to tolerate a large number of such intelligent failures. But loosely defined, insufficiently monitored experiments have a way of spinning out of control—those are the failures you have to be able to avoid.

How do you foster the former while avoiding the latter? Creating a psychologically safe organizational culture—one that's conducive to the questioning, information sharing, and risk taking that innovation requires—is crucial, but it can also take a while. Better to "start small, in the self-contained environment of your own unit," says

David A. Garvin, Robert and Jane Cizik Professor of Business Administration at Harvard Business School, and to establish ground rules for intelligent failure that can inform your experimentation while the cultural work proceeds.

Setting Boundaries

In *Leading the Revolution,* Gary Hamel, founder and chairman of the consulting firm Strategos and a visiting professor at the London Business School, makes a number of recommendations about how to engineer risk taking into your organization's DNA. Precisely because the failure rates are so high, he maintains, your innovation bank has to be stocked with lots of ideas, experiments, ventures, and new businesses. And you should manage each of these categories explicitly, the way a financial advisor manages an investment portfolio.

Useful advice, but it overlooks the other side of the coin. What companies need right now are guidelines to ensure that an experiment is worth the risk. "Intelligent failures minimize the organizational cost while maximizing the organizational learning," says Garvin. They have the following parameters:

* THEY START WITH PRIOR ASSUMPTIONS. "If you go into an experiment saying, 'Let's just see what happens,' or if you haven't written down

beforehand what your expectations are, it's unlikely that you'll learn anything from it," says Garvin. "You'll be too susceptible to what's called the hindsight bias—concluding that what happened in the experiment confirms what you were expecting all along."

- THEY'RE RELATIVELY SMALL. "Failures that are really big have too many political repercussions." People's careers are put at stake, and the resulting tumult prevents the organization from learning from the experience.

- THE FEEDBACK LOOP IS RELATIVELY SHORT. "It does you no good to launch a prototype and then wait three years to receive feedback about it. Market conditions and customers' needs will have changed too much in the interim. The ideal," says Garvin, "is to begin collecting information about your experiment within weeks, although some projects require longer."

Research on new-product development at Motorola (cell phones), General Electric (CAT scanners), Corning (optical fibers), and Searle (Nutrasweet) reveals the benefits of a "probe-and-learn process," a method of successive approximation through intelligent failure. As authors Gary S. Lynn, Joseph G. Morone, and Albert S. Paulson explain, these companies learned how to get the products right by bringing to market a product that was initially just good enough. They quickly refined the product in response to customers' comments and then iterated this feedback-and-improvement process numerous times.

The innovation and design services firm IDEO provides an excellent model for how to fail intelligently. "They've raised prototyping to the level of an art form," says Garvin. All their prototypes must meet what the company calls "the rule of the 3Rs": they must be rough (for example, a styrofoam model of a telephone handset can be made quickly and cheaply, but it still enables you to test the handset's ease of use), rapid, and right (close enough to the desired form, function, and performance features).

Parameters tied to cost and duration can also help ensure that your failures will be intelligent. "If you fail quickly and inexpensively, that's a good failure, particularly if you discover that the assumptions about how the market will change or how customers' needs will evolve don't hold," says John Wilson, manager of the Strategic Enterprise Fund (SEF), the private equity investment arm of UPS. He's not being facetious when he says that: the cost and the duration of the experiment are critical, but SEF doesn't set concrete, across-the-board targets for either. Part of the reason, says Wilson, is that, in contrast to many corporate venture-capital units, for whom financial returns are the highest priority, the SEF's primary mission is to bring knowledge back into the company. "We're looking to explore emerging technologies or new markets that have strategic importance to UPS's future," he explains. "Financial considerations are really at the bottom of our list of priorities." But they do come into play all the same. "We invest in the early stages of a start-up company, typically in the A or B round of financing. At that stage, the start-up's expertise is not widely known, so not only is the investment less expensive, there's also a greater upside potential."

Core competency figures prominently in UPS's deliberations about how to structure an experiment. If it falls within the company's core competencies, UPS's internal product development group tends to take responsibility for the project. But if the experiment is beyond those core competencies—say, developing software that could significantly improve UPS's service—the SEF helps those groups look for outside start-ups to invest in. The due-diligence process for vetting such partners includes such questions as, What will we learn from this investment that we wouldn't have learned otherwise? and, What is the viability of this start-up company's idea?

But perhaps the most important parameter UPS has, says Wilson, is the requirement that "each investment have an internal sponsor—some unit within the company that's willing to support the investment, usually by serving as an observer on the start-up's board." This stipulation ensures that the experiment is strategically important to UPS, thereby increasing the likelihood that the lessons learned—even if the experiment fails—will be valuable.

One such investment, in Moai Technologies, a maker of online auction software, has lost money. But the insights gained from the partnership have helped UPS improve the speed and efficiency of its own Web site. Another investment that's currently struggling involves HighPoint Systems, a maker of order-entry software that enables consumers to scan goods at home and create an online shopping list more easily. Investing in this start-up played a role in UPS's eventual determination that "the economics of home grocery delivery make it difficult for the delivery service provider to earn any money," says Wilson. The lessons learned helped UPS avoid a disastrous decision to enter that market, and depending on how the home office supply market develops, they may someday provide positive benefits as well, he adds. Although these investments haven't panned out from a

> Freedom to fail "should not be confused with a license to commit foolish mistakes."

financial perspective, they have boosted UPS's intellectual capital and helped it maintain a sound strategic course.

Investing in outside firms "lowers the personal risk to UPS employees," says Wilson, "because we're learning from the experience—and sometimes the failure—of entrepreneurs outside the company." If the experiment fails, it's less traumatic to write off the investment than it is to have to shut down an internal venture and lay off employees, he notes. That's true to a degree, but no company can survive by relying exclusively on outside partnerships or investments for all its innovation. Your internal culture needs to be supportive of calculated risk-taking activities.

Human psychology being what it is, most people tend to be overly optimistic about a project's chances of success going in. "You'd never get people to sign on to a difficult project if they didn't overinflate the odds of success," says Garvin. "Besides, in most instances, the project's riskiness doesn't become apparent until you're well under way."

Dorothy Leonard, William J. Abernathy Professor of Business Administration at Harvard Business School, agrees with Garvin's assessment. Nevertheless, she says, "it's important to make sure that the people above you in the organization understand there's some degree of risk associated with the project you're undertaking." Moreover, as she and coauthor Walter Swap note in *When Sparks Fly,* the composition and structure of your team should be matched to the degree of risk you're taking. With a project that's a big risk, for example, you're going to want a highly creative, intellectually diverse team and a team leader who's a heavyweight.

The Foundations of Psychological Safety

Does risk taking flourish only in a stress-free environment? Not according to Edmondson's study of a large public utility in the mid-Atlantic region. Under tremendous pressure to cut costs, this organization laid off 25% of its staff and still found novel ways to be more productive. Under a new CEO's leadership, the utility benchmarked best practices in similar organizations, eliminated an entire layer of management (mostly through generous early-retirement packages), boosted the pay of most remaining workers, and gave them greater decision-making flexibility by creating action teams charged with discovering cheaper ways of doing business.

The CEO's message to employees after the restructuring, was, says Edmondson, "'The situation is urgent, and we need *you* to turn it around.' He made it clear that the commission was in trouble and that things were going to have to change, but he also let the remaining workers know that they wouldn't be penalized for trying new approaches." This example underscores another hallmark of intelligent failures: they're nonpunitive. "Urgency and punishment really work at cross-purposes to each other, even if it doesn't seem that way at first," says Edmondson. "Employees can stand the pressure of declining revenues and the fear of impending job cuts as long as they are assured that their peers and bosses won't bite their heads off for taking appropriate risks."

One way to promote risk taking, writes Hamel, is to make sure that your company's metrics "focus as much on innovation and wealth creation as on optimization and wealth conservation." Another is to change your underlying assumptions about failure. "Most companies work on the assumption of perfection and infallibility," says Garvin. "They assume that if they're conducting 10 experiments, nine of them should be successful. But IDEO takes the position that if five of the 1,000 ideas it's testing pan out, that's an enormous success." You don't achieve excellence by planning for perfection—you do it by creating an environment that allows teams to make mistakes and to learn from them.

In "Speeding Up Team Learning" (*Harvard Business Review,* October 2001), a study of surgery teams' abilities to adapt to new technology that makes "minimally invasive cardiac surgery" possible, Edmondson and colleagues Richard Bohmer and Gary Pisano demonstrate how intelligent failure plays a role even in work where there's very little tolerance for error. "Much of the information about the patient's heart that the surgeon traditionally gleaned through sight and touch is now delivered via digital readouts and ultrasound images displayed on monitors out of his or her field of vision," they write. The teams that adapted to the new technology the fastest and the most effectively took advantage of trial and error. They were able to experiment "with new ways of doing things to improve team performance—even if some of the new ways turned out not to work." For these teams, such real-time learning "occasionally yielded insights that might have been lost had a team member waited" for a formal after-action review, which is such a critical part of much organizational learning. Indeed, a number of the practices that ended up being institutionalized as part of the new standard operating procedure were originally identified during the minute-by-minute reflection that characterizes a trial-and-error process.

Whereas the process of trial and error occurs in private when individuals learn, "on a team, people risk appearing ignorant or incompetent when they suggest or try something new," the authors continue. "Neutralizing the fear of embarrassment is necessary in order to achieve the robust back-and-forth communication" that innovation and real-time learning require. Here, the team leader's role is vital. On the most successful cardiac surgery teams, the authors found that the leaders served as "fallibility models": they were willing to admit their mistakes to the team. "The new technology requires team members to adopt a greater interdependence in order to work effectively," Edmondson explains. "With hierarchical teams, if you want everyone to be able to admit and discuss their errors when there's an opportunity to do so, if the leader isn't willing to go first, then the whole exercise is likely to fail."

When the leader models the assumption that failure is an inevitable part of the innovation process, everyone else on the team sees that it's really okay to make mistakes in the course of your work and to talk about them with your colleagues. They understand that real-time learning is a genuine organizational value, not just a snazzy catchphrase. But the freedom to fail "should not be confused with a license to commit foolish mistakes," writes Garvin in *Learning in Action.* "Accountability remains essential for effective performance, and no organization should embrace fuzzy or wrongheaded thinking. At GE, the difference is well understood. According to the head of leadership development: 'If your decision made sense, given the database you had at the time, you won't be hanged for it. If you made a bad decision and anyone could have foreseen it, nobody's very forgiving.'"

For Further Reading

Learning in Action: A Guide to Putting the Learning Organization to Work by David A. Garvin (2000, Harvard Business School Press)

When Sparks Fly: Igniting Creativity in Groups by Dorothy Leonard and Walter Swap (1999, Harvard Business School Press)

Leading the Revolution by Gary Hamel (2000, Harvard Business School Press)

"Marketing and Discontinuous Innovation: The Probe and Learn Process" by Gary S. Lynn, Joseph G. Morone, and Albert S. Paulson (*California Management Review,* 1996)

Reprint U0201B

Five Steps to Thriving in Times of Uncertainty

• • •

Peter Jacobs

In times of rapid change and heightened uncertainty, seemingly solid business strategies can derail with astounding speed. An unforeseen competitor enters the market with a cheaper product; consumer tastes shift rapidly to a new technology; world events conspire to throttle your access to key resources. The possibilities for strategic disruption seem endless.

For a company to thrive today, its managers must find ways to increase their units' and the organization's ability to read and react to industry and market changes. Their goal: to boost the company's strategic flexibility by learning how to see potential disruptions earlier and respond faster.

For most companies, this does not come easily, note Katsuhiko Shimizu of the University of Texas, San Antonio, and Michael Hitt of Texas A&M University.

In a 2004 *Academy of Management Executive* article, Shimizu and Hitt bring into clear focus the barriers companies face in building strategic flexibility and identify several steps managers can take to overcome them. Their ideas, combined with the insights of other experts and top executives, provide a valuable framework for increasing your company's strategic flexibility.

The Critical Ability to Confront Change and Uncertainty

Shimizu and Hitt define strategic flexibility as an organization's capacity to:

- Identify major changes in its external environments.

- Quickly commit resources to new courses of action in response to such changes.

- Recognize and act promptly when it's time to halt or reverse existing resource commitments.

The dynamic competitive landscape of recent years has made speed a critical component of each of these capabilities.

Consider Polaroid. The former king of instant photography took years to acknowledge and respond to the advances of digital imaging. By the time the company finally did, it was too little, too late.

Whether Polaroid was blind to industry changes, opted to ignore them, or lacked the resources to respond effectively is unclear. However, the company exemplifies what Hitt suggests is a kind of strategic rigidity. Whatever its corporate strategy may have been, Polaroid seemed steadfastly committed to that strategy even while technological advances rendered it irrelevant.

It's easy enough to scoff at Polaroid's apparent incompetence, but how prepared is your company to deal with the unforeseen?

Five Steps to Maintain Strategic Flexibility

Because managers at every level are subject to psychological and organizational biases, maintaining strategic flexibility is seldom a simple task. The following steps, however, will help.

1. Measure and monitor outcomes.

At Dow Corning Corporation, the senior management team reviews the strategic performance of each major corporate initiative at least quarterly. "In reality, monitoring is even more fluid because we meet frequently to review and evaluate project performance against designated targets," says Scott Fuson, Dow Corning's chief marketing officer. "Dow Corning is involved in dozens of diverse markets where everything changes constantly, so close monitoring is essential to keep projects on track and within budget."

It is also important, Shimizu and Hitt note, for organizations to think hard about what they measure. For example, if your goal is to capture market share from a rival, you can't just measure total sales because the market might well have grown and, with it, your rival's sales as well. Similarly, if you are shifting focus to new growth initiatives, you can't rely on metrics meant to monitor the success of fully mature businesses.

To further boost organizational adaptability, Fuson advises companies to keep projects affordable and flexible, committing resources to new initiatives one stage at a time—especially at the beginning. "If monitoring suddenly indicates a major change in direction is likely to significantly improve project outcome but the budget is already stretched to its limit, the whole initiative could be at risk," he explains.

2. Have someone play devil's advocate.

Leaders need to be aware of their own cognitive biases, lest they get stuck in a too-rigid way of looking at the world. Designating a trusted associate—or, better yet, more than one—to assume the role of devil's advocate within your team is an excellent way, Shimizu and Hitt note, to uncover our biases.

What about nonteam decisions? Hitt finds that, for lack of time, managers often make key strategic decisions themselves. But even then, he says, sharing your thinking with colleagues and seeking their feedback can help you keep a truly open mind.

The main obstacle to devil's advocacy is our natural reluctance to being viewed as a naysayer. The authors point to General Motors as a telling example. When Roger Smith manned GM's helm, anyone who voiced a problem was quickly dubbed as negative and not a team player. Debra Meyerson, an associate professor at Stanford University's School of Education and (by courtesy) its Graduate School of Business, and author of *Tempered Radicals: How Everyday Leaders Inspire Change at Work,* says companies need to encourage people to voice their views even if they disagree with the dominant perspective. "Organizations can't learn if everyone thinks and speaks in the same tongue," she says.

3. Pursue external perspectives.

Listening with an open mind to the thoughts and ideas of those with differing viewpoints, whether from outside a particular business unit or outside the company altogether, is another effective way of countering management biases. Typically unnoticed, biases such as a tendency to overlook negative feedback or to act too

Making Your Organization Change-Ready

To achieve strategic flexibility, organizations must embrace change as an inevitable and essential part of an organization's growth.

But few corporate leaders do. Indeed, even in unpredictable business climates, managers tend to focus almost all their energy on successfully executing the current strategy. What they also should be doing is preparing for an unknown future.

The essential first step in this effort is to ensure the company is change-ready at all times—that is, to ensure that the people within the organization are prepared for and capable of shifting what they do, how they do it, and with whom they do it.

If such a mindset is not already in place in your company or unit, there are certain steps you can take.

Challenge Complacency

It's difficult to motivate people to change when they are satisfied with their current situation. Explain why change will inevitably be necessary and provide the relevant information to make employees understand.

Give Your Employees a Voice

Employees who can freely express their ideas—and who think you will listen to them—will feel more empowered to act. Encourage open discussions about the change program, and work to understand resistance by exploring people's concerns. When people believe their voice matters, they are more apt to mobilize for change.

Encourage Participative Work

Develop more participative approaches to how everyday business is handled, specifically:

- Bring decision making down to the lowest levels possible.
- Keep the lines of communication open.
- Share information freely.
- Familiarize yourself with the issues faced by frontline employees.
- Focus on building collaboration through cross-functional teams.

Drive Fear Out of Your Group

Fear encourages people to avoid risks, become internally focused, and stop communicating. It also costs organizations real money in terms of reduced productivity and diminished quality of work. Aim to reduce fear, but do not deny the challenges that come with change. Employees at all levels in the organization must feel free to identify problems and suggest solutions. They must also feel free to experiment and try new things without fear of retribution if they fail.

—Siobhan Ford

Adapted from *Harvard Business Essentials: Manager's Toolkit—The 13 Skills Managers Need to Succeed* (Harvard Business School Press, 2004) and *Harvard ManageMentor.*

swiftly grow entrenched over time, especially if management turnover is low. Shimizu and Hitt say obtaining fresh external insight is therefore important at every organizational level. Consider the following steps companies can take to help make it happen:

- ROUTINELY APPOINT OUTSIDE BOARD MEMBERS. New external directors are obliged to learn about the company and, in the process, tend to question policies and practices long taken for granted.

- LIMIT TOP EXECUTIVES' TENURE. "Arrival of a new outside CEO," the authors say, "provides an opportunity for an organization to revisit old assumptions and correct mistakes in past strategic decisions." For example, despite their outstanding performance, the last two CEOs of Toyota stepped down after four and six years, respectively.

- ROTATE MANAGERS ROUTINELY. Many organizations rotate certain managers and executives as part of their training programs, but other companies leave the same people in the same positions for years. Stale thinking and inertia inevitably result. Conversely, cross-training not only broadens an organization's knowledge and skills but it also energizes and motivates participants.

- EXPLOIT PARTNER ALLIANCES. Alliances with other firms have become popular strategic moves, usually as a way to mutually capitalize on complementary resources. However, such alliances can also be excellent sources of fresh ideas, insight, and learning.

- CREATE AD HOC ADVISORY GROUPS. A CEO or business unit leader will often assemble an informal group to help analyze and assess the potential outcomes of important strategic decisions—for example, whether and what the firm should outsource and to which vendor. Leaders must be clear on their expectations for what the group will provide and in what form. Advisory-group participants are most often managers chosen to reflect a broad cross section of expertise.

Shimizu and Hitt concede that their suggestions involve some disadvantages and risk. New executives and managers, for instance, might reshape currently effective strategies simply to add their own distinct mark. The learning curve for anyone in a new job also must be a consideration.

"Be careful about external viewpoints," cautions Steve Odland, chairman and CEO of Office Depot. "Those who don't fully understand your organization can lead you off track and destroy your brand proposition. Strategic inconsistency can confuse customers and, ultimately, destroy shareholder value. Maintaining balance is therefore critical."

4. View decisions as a portfolio of options.

Organizations usually have multiple projects and initiatives under way simultaneously, and it's critical that leaders not let one or two dominate their attention. As markets shift, seemingly less significant initiatives may quickly become the most valuable.

One way to maintain a balanced perspective, Shimizu and Hitt note, is to periodically review the organization's projects and initiatives as a portfolio of options. Doing so makes it easier to reallocate resources from one project to another offering even greater promise given the state of the market.

Smaller organizations tend to have fewer initiatives under way simultaneously but can easily expand their decision portfolios by including small variations and experiments.

5. Analyze outcomes and apply learning.

Flexibility stems from the ability to learn. But do companies learn all they can from the strategic initiatives they undertake? Probably not. Managers tend to overlook the negative and emphasize the positive. However, only by carefully examining what has led to negative outcomes as well as positive ones can managers maximize their learning experience.

If a corporate acquisition performs poorly, for example, but management learns a lot from the experience, the company can divest the asset and apply its newfound knowledge to make future acquisitions more successful. Or, if the company's executive team senses the problem stems from ineffective integration, it can postpone divestiture until it better understands the problem.

Determining the specific value of such learning may not be possible, but companies ought to consider it as part of every project's return on investment. Often, it will change their perspective significantly.

A good example, Shimizu and Hitt note, is Cisco Systems. The company has grown considerably through a series of successful acquisitions. The authors found Cisco makes a concerted effort to learn as much as possible from each acquisition, and takes great care to avoid the departure of key personnel who possess significant knowledge about the acquired company, its industries, and its markets. These employees can become powerful teachers, helping organizations to see their business and their markets in a new light. The ability to adopt such new perspectives is, of course, a critical element in building strategic flexibility.

Reprint U0512A

Web Services

Technology as a Catalyst
for Strategic Thinking

* * *

John Hagel III

As financial pressures mount, companies are looking for relief from the rigid, high-cost infrastructures that make cost reduction and growth such daunting challenges. Increasingly, their ability to deliver additional rounds of cost savings and to improve their return on assets depends on greater flexibility and an enhanced ability to collaborate.

A new generation of information technology–related architectures—known variously as Web services technology or distributed service architectures—can help managers meet these challenges.

Unlike the first generation of Web, which focused on connecting people to Web sites, Web services technology

> If we've learned anything, it's that technology is at best a catalyst or enabler, not an answer in itself.

automates connections across applications and data—without human intervention. More than "just another IT investment," this next generation of IT can be the catalyst for an overhaul of management thinking.

Web services are often confused with application service providers (ASPs), which use a "rental" pricing model and shared-services delivery to make traditional application software available to a broader range of customers. Although Web services also are made available to users as shared services, they solve many of the problems associated with ASPs—most notably, the difficulties in service delivery caused by reliance on very traditional software technology.

Web services technology represents a major step forward in the ongoing effort to generate business value from IT: it does not require the removal of the extensive IT infrastructures that companies have accumulated

Defining Web Services

In an effort to merge all their disparate and proprietary IT systems, many big companies invested giant sums of money over the past few years in huge, complex, enterprise-resource-planning systems. These ERPs, which offer suites of interlinked applications that draw on unified databases, solve some problems, but most companies still struggle with a hodgepodge of hundreds of incompatible systems. Because these systems are relatively inflexible, they tend to lock companies into rigid business processes.

Web services architecture, constructed on the Internet, is an open rather than proprietary architecture. Instead of building and maintaining unique internal systems, companies can rent the functionality they need—whether it's data storage, processing power, or specific applications.

At work are three layers of technology:

- First, at the foundation are the software standards and communication protocols, such as XML and SOAP, that allow information to be exchanged easily among different applications. These tools provide the common languages for Web services, so applications can connect freely and read electronic messages. This means that information management is dramatically streamlined—the IT department doesn't have to write customized code whenever communication with a new application is needed.

- Second, the service grid, the middle layer of the architecture, builds upon the protocols and standards. Like an electrical power grid, the service grid provides a set of shared utilities—from security to third-party auditing to billing and payment—that makes it possible to carry out business functions and transactions over the Internet. In addition, the service grid encompasses a set of utilities, usually supplied and managed by third parties, that facilitates the transport of messages (such as routing and filtering), the identification of available services (such as directories and brokers), and the assurance of reliability and consistency.

Thus the grid plays two key roles: helping Web services users and providers find and connect with ease and creating trusted environments to carry out mission-critical business activities. A robust service grid is vital to accelerating and broadening the potential impact of Web services. Without it, Web services remain relatively marginal.

- Third, the top layer of the architecture comprises a diverse area of application services, from credit card processing to production scheduling, that automate particular business functions. It is this layer that day to day will be most visible to employees and customers. Some application services will be proprietary to a particular company or group of firms, while others will be shared among all companies.

  In some cases, companies may develop their own application services and then choose to sell them on a subscription basis to other enterprises.

over the decades. Instead, it provides an overlay that can connect IT platforms more quickly and more cost-effectively than previous generations of technology could.

Such a connecting overlay substantially reduces IT development and operating costs—but that is only a small part of Web service technology's usefulness. Its real value lies in increased flexibility and collaboration, which in turn generate significant operating savings and growth options across the entire business. For example, by finding new ways to work together, companies can both eliminate substantial inefficiencies and mobilize a broader range of resources to deliver greater value to customers.

If we've learned anything since the 1980s, it's that technology is at best a catalyst and an enabler—it's never an answer in itself. Too often, managers eager to reap significant economic benefits have purchased technology, only to find that the rewards fell short of expectations: the additional operating cost and capital expense did not produce a corresponding performance improvement or return on investment.

Executives have learned their lesson; they avoid the temptation to inject technology into the business without changing the business at the same time. They understand that to harness the capability of Web services for greater flexibility and collaboration, they need to rethink some of the most basic questions of all, such as "What business are we really in?" and "What is the nature of the enterprise?"

Fortunately, using Web services does not require massive overnight change. Nor is it about creating new business on a greenfield basis. Instead, the idea is to reshape existing businesses one step at a time, so as to realize additional value from existing assets.

For instance, Dell Computer now uses Web services to connect with suppliers and third-party logistics providers. General Motors has started at the other end of the business, using Web services to coordinate its interactions with dealers and auto purchasers. Over time, GM plans to use a consortium it established with Ford and Daimler-Chrysler to extend this technology architecture to its relationships with suppliers.

We've all grown tired of the "change-the-world promises" of new technology—and the concomitant demand for massive capital infusions over extended periods of time. Today, the proposition is far more pragmatic: invest modest sums and insist on near-term economic returns. Don't move forward unless these results materialize. When they do, you'll soon realize that the intensifying competition will force you to expand the implementation of the technology to other areas of your business and to rethink your business to generate even greater near-term economic benefit. Over time, the cumulative impact will be profound.

Reprint U0211D

Strategies for Growing Your Company

. . .

Many corporate strategies have growth—in sales, revenues, profitability, market share, and other dimensions—as their ultimate objective. For that reason, the articles in this section focus on strategies for spurring and maintaining growth. In the pages that follow, you'll find guidelines for increasing sales as well as sustaining profitable growth by expanding into businesses related closely to your company's core. The section concludes with an article summing up powerful growth strategies offered in three books on the subject.

How Strategic Is Your Sales Strategy?

• • •

Theodore Kinni

Bringing high-level corporate strategy to the ground-level sales effort is a challenge for most organizations. Yes, most high-performing sales teams do carry with them a solid sense of company goals and priorities, but a sizable gap can exist between the way strategy is implemented in most parts of the organization and its role in sales. And into that gap falls a great deal of potential value. Recognizing that, some companies are infusing their sales efforts with a more vigorous sense of strategy and unveiling promising new methodologies in the process.

Putting the Right People in the Right Seats

In *Good to Great,* Jim Collins tells managers to get "the right people on the bus, the wrong people off the bus, and the right people in the right seats." Could there be any business area in which this advice is more critical than sales? After all, selling is among the most "people" of all people functions.

"Hiring the right people in sales is very challenging. Unless you are very strategic, at best, you may be 50-50," says Larry MacGirr, vice president of sales for North America for CIBA Vision.

To increase the odds, the contact lens maker developed a profiling instrument that attempts to match the personality traits of prospective account executives with those found in the company's top performers. Echoing Collins's belief that companies should put more emphasis on "character attributes" than on specific experience, skills, or background, CIBA Vision worked with Profiles International to establish the baseline personality traits of its "eagles"—the top 20% of its sales team. The resulting profile then became the basis of a tool CIBA Vision uses when hiring. Seeking specific traits in new hires "gives us the type of people we need to be successful," says MacGirr. "We then put new hires into our training program and develop their skills to as high a level as possible."

Developing effective sales managers is another CIBA Vision priority. As with its eagles, CIBA Vision profiled its best frontline sales managers and created a tool for evaluating candidates for managerial positions. The company soon recognized that individual sales success is not a defining indicator of management potential. In seeking sales managers, MacGirr says, "I am not necessarily looking for my top performers as much as I am looking for my top performers who are able to influence their peers."

So how can you retain high performers who aren't destined to manage? You provide them "another career path that keeps them selling," says MacGirr. At CIBA Vision "supersellers" may be given the large driver accounts. For those who won't become managers, "we will give you opportunities to have a bigger impact on the marketplace and on the company as your skills and abilities grow as a seller."

Segmenting on Needs and Priorities

In 2001, when Hill-Rom Company, a $1.2 billion maker of patient-care products, decided to rethink its sales effort, the company looked first at its segmentation strategy. Like many companies, Hill-Rom had been segmenting its customers by size. But after analyzing a variety of customer characteristics—including capital spending, profit margins, occupancy rates, and so forth—and

What Are the Real Drivers of Sales Performance?

Andy Zoltners, professor of marketing at Northwestern University's Kellogg School of Management, says that many executives ignore most of the real drivers of sales performance. Instead, they typically look to improve performance through training or compensation.

But neither approach will "fix problems like the sales force not being structured properly or people located in the wrong places or poor frontline management," says Zoltners.

How do you avoid the trap? "Spend a lot of time working issues back to the drivers to figure out which ones are going to matter," he says.

In his book *The Complete Guide to Accelerating Sales Force Performance,* Zoltners identifies these four categories of sales-performance drivers:

Sales Research

Market understanding, define needs
>Market segmentation
>Market assessment
>Market prioritization
>Market targeting

People

Selling competencies
>Recruiting
>Training
>Promotions

Coaching
Supervision

Motivation

Evaluation
Progression

Sales Systems

Compensation

Incentives
Benefits
Provide data
Lead generation
Targeting
Provide tools
Precision selling
Automation

Investment and Organization

Size

Structure
Deployment
Product
Market
Activity
Territory alignment
Sales and marketing coordination
Provide processes
Strategic selling
Mentoring
Partnering
Consultative selling

interviews with salespeople and customers, Hill-Rom found that it could better serve its customers using a segmentation strategy that focused not on their size but on their needs and priorities.

The new strategy led Hill-Rom to recast its customer base into two broad groups, which the company termed *key* and *prime* customers. Key customers purchased with greater frequency and tended to buy suites of products. Prime customers were more concerned with price and tended to purchase individual products. Hill-Rom also found that selling to prime customers cost four to five times as much as selling to key customers.

When the company implemented a new sales approach and structure based on the new segments, sales effectiveness quickly improved. In a year, the company's revenue growth rate doubled, sales rose in both segments, and overall customer satisfaction increased 6%. Meanwhile, over two years, the cost of sales dropped 1% each year.

"Amazingly enough, a large number of companies are still working in a world where doing customer segmentation means breaking your customers up by large, medium, and small," says Mike Weissel, a director at the consultancy Mercer Oliver Wyman. Instead, Weissel recommends segmentation that encompasses both demographic and behavioral factors. "The behavioral piece of that allows you to understand buying behaviors and both the relative value today and the potential value of customers in the future," he says. "The demographic piece allows you to find the customers. The key when you talk about sales force effectiveness is the ability to take segmentation all the way down to tagging individual customers."

Building a Sales Process Around Diagnosis

High-performing sellers can expend as much effort in helping customers understand their own needs and problems as they do in pitching their wares. This diagnostic approach is especially valuable in such industries as high tech, professional services, and health care, says Jeff Thull, author of *Mastering the Complex Sale.* "In a complex environment, customers need expert help to understand their problems and the parameters of an effective solution," says Thull. "Buying is decision making, and the salesperson who guides the customer through a high-quality decision process is perceived as a valued business partner instead of a self-serving piranha."

The Graham Company, a commercial insurance broker, brings the value of diagnosis into sharp relief. Graham is the 51st-largest insurance broker in the United States, reporting an annual premium volume of more than $200 million, yet its sales force represents less than 10% of its nearly 170 employees, and it generates its premiums from only 200 corporate clients. (Its nearest competitors have 2,000 to 3,000 clients.)

Graham's approach is a radical departure from tradition. In an industry in which selling is a numbers game (provide enough attractive quotes and you'll win your share), the company invests in a highly selective process of new client discovery. In each of the last several years, it typically contacted only 350 prospective clients, decided to seek a relationship with only 35 of those prospects, and earned the business of 28.

In pursuing clients, Graham invests substantial resources diagnosing the customer's situation. The brokerage sends a team, which can include attorneys, risk managers, engineers, CPAs, and experts in the customer's business, to evaluate the prospect's insurance issues and exposures. This work is provided free as part of the sales process. (Consultants might charge $75,000 for comparable work.)

Similarly, Graham pursues an engagement with its clients that is deeper than that of the traditional insurance model. The company involves itself in the ongoing alignment of risk management strategies with the customer's business objectives—for example, reviewing the insurance issues of proposed acquisitions.

How well does such a selling strategy work? Graham enjoys a 75% conversion rate in an industry with a 15% average and maintains a 98% customer retention rate.

Three years ago, Waters Corporation, an $890 million maker of analytic instrumentation, also adopted a diagnosis-based sales process. "One of the fundamental differences between other sales approaches and diagnostic selling is the notion that buying and changing are, in fact, similar processes," says Richard Brooks, vice president of Americas Marketing. "If you understand how difficult it is to change, then you automatically understand how difficult the buying process is.

"Another important difference is the relationship of the whole process to the cost of [the] customer's problem. It's not so easy to do, but when you really help a customer understand the cost of their problem, it makes it easier for them to choose an expensive solution as long as they can see it is cost-effective," Brooks says.

"You want to spend about 35% to 40% of your time with a customer developing that customer's needs," says CIBA Vision's MacGirr. "Once you get the need well defined and established in both of your minds, the next step is not to present, but to confirm the need. Once that's done, the close is actually pretty quick."

Reprint U0402B

Creative Destruction or Concentrating on the Core

Which Is the Right Path to Growth?

• • •

Adrian Mello

The torpid global economy has companies panting for new profit opportunities. But this comes at a time when "the odds against winning the growth game are worse than ever," says Chris Zook, a director at the management consulting firm Bain & Co.

S&P 500 price-earnings ratios, which have consistently stayed over 20, reflect shareholders' continuing unrealistic expectations about future growth. Such high P/E ratios are unprecedented in a recession, notes Zook, particularly in a world-synchronized recession that spans the top 10 economies. Moreover, investors are shifting in and out of stocks at five times the rate they did a few decades ago, giving management teams greatly reduced time frames in which to produce growth.

> Devotion to past success can ossify an organization.

Zook's extensive research points to a relentless focus on the company's core businesses as the best way to achieve growth in these difficult times. His counterpart at McKinsey & Co., Richard Foster, has also studied the problem of growth in depth. In 1917, he notes, the 100 largest American companies were ranked and celebrated in the Forbes 100 list. When Forbes revisited the list in 1987, it found that 61 of the original companies had gone the way of the dinosaur. Of the 39 that had survived, only 18 were still among the top 100. Even more startling, these 18 companies earned a return on investment that was 20% less than the overall market during the same time period—and only two, General Electric and Eastman Kodak, generated a return better than the market average.

Big corporations are designed for continuity, not change, Foster continues. Corporate structures, processes, and decision making all support maintaining consistency over extended periods of time in order to optimize continuing operations. Building the corporation for continuous operations may have made sense at one time, notes Foster, coauthor with Sarah Kaplan of *Creative Destruction: Why Companies That Are Built to Last Underperform the Market—And How to Successfully Transform Them.* But the rate of change has accelerated dramatically, rendering the old corporate design unfit for rapid sustainable growth. To keep pace, companies must continually reinvent themselves—sometimes exiting successful businesses in order to move into more profitable ones.

As divergent as Foster's and Zook's recommendations may first seem, further investigation reveals areas of agreement, especially when it comes to expanding—or even changing—what your company does best. But first, a little background about the thinking behind each approach.

Growing from the Core

A foundation for growth starts with a clear definition of a company's core business, says Zook. The reason: the core is the most likely source of profit. Most companies that sustain value creation over time, he adds, have only one or two strong cores. In *Profit from the Core: Growth Strategy in an Era of Turbulence,* Zook and coauthor James Allen explain that a core business involves one or more of the following:

- Your most strategically significant "franchise" customers (those who have the highest profit potential)

- Your most differentiated and strategic capabilities

- Your most critical product offerings

- Your most important channels

- Other critical strategic assets, such as key patents or brands.

If the biggest pitfall to growth is the failure to define a core business, the next biggest is the premature abandonment of a core business. Beware the siren song that urges you to "discard the old, leave your historic core business behind and set out for the promised land," warns Zook.

After carefully growing its optics business for 120 years, Bausch & Lomb purchased a breakthrough patent that helped it capture the market for soft contact lenses.

When competitors began attacking its position, Bausch & Lomb sought new sources of growth in such products as electric toothbrushes, skin ointments, and hearing aids, which had no obvious link to the core. Deprived of resources and management's attention, the contact lens business flattened out. Bausch & Lomb's stock dropped significantly; the one-time market leader fell to third place behind Johnson & Johnson and Ciba Vision.

What Creative Destruction Does and Doesn't Mean

Large companies tend to enshrine their past success and institutionalize it, assuming that what worked well in the past will lead to future success, says Foster. But devotion to past success only ossifies the organization, robbing it of the flexibility it needs to adapt to an increasingly turbulent business environment.

"However hard it is to create a new business, it's harder to get rid of one that you already have," Foster says. Embracing new opportunities can sometimes require jettisoning established wisdom about how to run a business, or even divesting a long-standing but now underperforming operation.

Nevertheless, Foster agrees with Zook that corporations should generally pursue opportunities that align with their core competencies. "IBM shouldn't go into health care and Johnson & Johnson shouldn't go into computers," he says. "I'm not saying companies have to radically change or totally transform their businesses, or die. What I am saying—the message of my book—is that if corporations want to perform at market levels, then they have to change at the pace and scale of their markets without losing control."

Moving Beyond the Core

Too much insistence on core competences, however, can make the corporation rigid and unreceptive to promising new opportunities, Foster continues. For his part, Zook acknowledges that as important as it is to focus on your core business, this may not always be sufficient to ensure sustainable growth. "Management teams constantly meet with opportunities to move into related businesses, and at times such moves are absolutely necessary to strengthen the core and add new profit streams," write Zook and Allen. Among the most difficult challenges a management team faces are choosing expansion opportunities. A paradox of growth, says Zook, is that "the stronger your core business, the more opportunities you have both to move into profitable adjacencies [businesses that are closely related to your core] and to lose focus."

Before evaluating adjacencies, make sure you have a clearly defined core, advises Zook. Then look for the opportunities nearby with the most potent sources of competitive differentiation and advantage—for example, new products, new channels, new customer segments, new geographies, new value chain steps, new technologies, and new businesses.

Keep an eye on the peripheries, recommends Foster. For example, if you're in retail, consider businesses that share customer bases or manufacturing processes with your core.

> The stronger your core, the more opportunities you have to move into profitable adjacencies—and the easier it is to lose focus.

But even exploring adjacencies isn't always enough, Zook admits. Turbulent industry change—new governmental regulations or technology that creates a new low-cost business model—may require a fundamental redefinition of your core.

"Some 5% to 7% of the companies on the S&P 500 fall off the list in any given year," says Foster. The core of the economy shifts over time—it's unreasonable for a company to think that it doesn't have to shift at a similar pace. So if your core is the rebar market, then you're clearly not performing at market levels—you'll have to shift your core if you hope to.

"Thirty years ago, Pfizer was a chemical company that did a small amount of business with pharmaceutical intermediates. Today, its core is in pharmaceuticals," continues Foster. "Kimberly-Clark caused an outcry when it sold off its paper mills, the historical core of the business. But that enabled a move into consumer paper and woven paper products—more profitable markets than those the company had been in before."

Creative destruction, in other words, serves as a vital complement to a focus on your core. According to its chairman, Scott Cook, Intuit represents a company that blends Foster's approach with Zook's. Intuit's track record of continually identifying unmet customer needs testifies to its ability to creatively destroy its business. Moving beyond its initial market for personal finance software, the company created easy-to-use versions of tax-preparation software and, later, financial software for small businesses. And although Cook eschews the language of focusing on the core, he analyzes issues in terms of what the company does best: "We don't define our core business because as soon as you do that you've limited your thinking," he says. "We've instead focused on the customer: Where are the unsolved problems we can solve well? And the second test for our business is: In which businesses do we think we can build durable competitive advantage?"

Perhaps Intuit's integration of creative-destruction thinking with a what's-my-core-competence perspective falls short of textbook seamless. But as long as it helps the company build durable competitive advantage, isn't that what it's all about?

Reprint U0301D

The Latest Thinking on Growth

• • •

Among certain circles that think about trends in management, a consensus has begun to emerge that the Next Big Thing is growth. Companies have put themselves through the "re-" exercises, goes the theory, reengineering or restructuring with varying degrees of success. Now they are realizing that they cannot downsize their way to glory. As a result, these days no self-respecting consulting firm is without an initiative to figure out "how to achieve simultaneous top- and bottom-line growth," as one participant in the exercise puts it.

Currently arriving in bookstores near you are the first fruits of this effort, three books by consultants that, at least according to their titles and subtitles, point to the higher road. Robert Tomasko's *Go for Growth!* offers

"Five Paths to Profit and Success." *Customer Centered Growth* by Richard Whiteley and Diane Hessan advertises "Five Proven Strategies for Building Competitive Advantage." Dwight Gertz and João P. A. Baptista, apparently not believers in the magic of five, chart three master strategies for getting bigger and richer in *Grow to Be Great*.

Alas, while each tome contains some provocative ideas—about which, more below—none actually tells you how to grow a company, if by that we mean taking an established organization and increasing its sales and profits step by step. Author Tomasko is straightforward about this omission, albeit only after the reader has made it through some 270 pages: "This is a direction-setting book," he writes. "The focus is on what to do, not how to do it." True for all these works, it turns out.

Let's not be too hard on the authors, however; the fault is not entirely theirs. The first major piece of learning to take away from their research is that achieving sustained profitable growth is tough. Indeed it may be the toughest managerial act in corporate America today. Gertz and Baptista have particularly good evidence on the point. From 1983 to 1993, only about 30% of Fortune 1000 companies managed 10% compound annual growth in revenues, they found. For the Fortune 500 industrials as a whole, inflation-adjusted CAGR was –.33, for the Service 500, 2.2%, good by comparison to the industrials but not so good compared to the overall economy, which grew at a 2.8% rate.

On the other, brighter hand, Gertz and Baptista knock in the head the myths that big companies can't grow—think of Hewlett-Packard, Motorola, or Wal-Mart—that being in a lousy industry must necessarily hold you back, and that once your company reaches a certain size its best hope to get bigger lies in acquisitions.

So how do you grow? Sifting and sorting among the three books, a reader can identify at least four generic strategies.

Grow by selling ever more to the same base of carefully selected customers

This is the strategy Gertz and Baptista call "customer franchise management," and it is just about the whole story in *Customer Centered Growth*. It reflects the realization, growing in popularity, that a company's most valuable asset may be the relationships it has with its existing customers.

The component elements of such a strategy, while familiar, are worth repeating: Look hard at your current pool of customers and decide which you want to continue to serve. You may find that only 20% represent 60% of your profits and that selling to the rest is more trouble than they're worth, particularly if they require a lot of attention or are not with you for the long haul.

When you have identified your target customers, ask yourself and your colleagues, "What are we selling?" Then consult the customers: "What are you buying?" As Whiteley and Hessan observe, "We usually think we're selling products and services. But our customers are buying the benefits they get from using our products and services, things like security, improved productivity, self-image, reputation."

Once you're clear on what you're purveying, you can really get cranking, at least according to Whiteley and Hessan's slightly hyperventilatory framework. Develop a "laser-beam focus" on your selected market, with an eye toward delivering unique value even as your customers' tastes change. Consider outsourcing what you can't do best. Instead of merely listening, "hardwire" into your business system the voice of the customer with maps of their expectations and "dynamic business scorecards" that reflect not just financials but also measures of customer satisfaction and product success. To ensure a long-term lock on the market, create a "proprietary customer interaction process that is as much a part of what [your] brand stands for as the core product itself." That one concept, "proprietary customer interaction process," and the ideas its discussion should spark, may alone justify laying out the $25 for *Customer Centered Growth*.

Just about everybody's favorite paragon of this strategy is USAA, which began selling auto insurance to military officers and now provides them a full port-folio of financial services, to the tune of $6 billion a year.

Grow by systematically cooking up new products or services

As Gertz and Baptista explain, on this front the significant corporate learning of the past 30 years comes in the "systematically" part of the formula. They describe how advances in project management, risk reduction, and time-to-market thinking have coalesced in some companies that now "excel at the rapid and continuous introduction of whole families of successful new products and services," a strategy the authors characterize as "moving the entire pipeline faster."

To make this work, it isn't enough for a company to manage an individual project well; there must also be a corporate infrastructure capable of supporting multiple projects simultaneously. Tell-tale signs that you have the whole act together include a pattern of completing projects on time and within budget, and a higher than average percentage of projects that make it into the advanced development stage. According to *Grow to Be Great,* recent champions of the form include Gillette, 3M, and, maybe best of all, Hewlett-Packard.

Establish control of a market, and then grow as it grows

If you want proof of this strategy's effectiveness, just look at Intel, Microsoft, or the Walt Disney Co., argues Robert Tomasko.

At the heart of his *Go for Growth!* are profiles of five different types of company, which he labels rule breakers (the old Apple Computer, Silicon Graphics), game players (Coca-Cola, PepsiCo), rule makers (see preceding paragraph), specialists (Batesville Casket, Midwest Express), and improvisers (America Online, the new Apple Computer). Tomasko richly describes the mindset that impels each type, their competitive strengths and weaknesses, and even what it feels like—good and bad— to work at one. The darkest shadings go to those control freaks, the rule makers, which makes the chapter on them particularly gripping.

Such companies may be present at the creation of their markets, but they typically don't make their move until "technologies and buying preferences settle down," Tomasko notes. Then they step in and set the standards for the industry—Microsoft's DOS operating system for PCs, Intel's X86 series of microprocessors—"often, but not always a result of having triumphed in a war for market share." Masters at thinking the game through several moves in advance, they look for potential chokepoints in the paths down which the industry is headed, then seek to position themselves at those chokepoints, if necessary by acquiring nascent companies that have the requisite technology. Rule makers are quite willing to cannibalize their old products with new offerings if that's what it takes to maintain control, their superordinate goal in life.

But years of market dominance can breed a self-blinding smugness, especially to radically new, transformative technologies. Irreverent Tomasko points out that in some sense, the Microsoft of the 1950s was General Motors; the Intel of the 1970s, IBM.

Grow by rethinking how you get your service or product to customers

Gertz and Baptista label this strategy channel management and see it as taking one of three forms: creating or exploiting wholly new channels (Dell Computer selling PCs over the phone); in effect becoming the channel, sucking up much of the profit that used to go to manufacturers or less efficient middlemen (Home Depot in building materials, Staples in office supplies); or simply getting better at exploiting your existing channel (Paychex in small business payroll processing).

It's under channel management that the authors of *Grow to Be Great* locate what might, to the untutored eye, seem the two most obvious paths to growth for many American companies in the late 20th century: selling more goods and services abroad (follow McDonald's or Coca-Cola, or join the legions dreaming of a piece of the action in the Wal-Martization of retailing worldwide) and selling via the technologies that make up the core infrastructure of the new economy.

> Companies like Intel look for chokepoints and then try to position themselves there.

Examples of successful growth companies abound in these three books, but for all the instruction and inspiration they provide, we're largely left with the question "How, exactly, do I get my organization on the path to growth?" An adequate answer would address a number of subsidiary issues, including: How do you change the minds, hearts, and behavior that result from waves of cost-cutting? In a restructured company, where do you find the animal spirits necessary to lead the charge? And how do you handle the difficult internal negotiations that arise when it becomes apparent to management that a growth initiative may require real live investment dollars? ("We know we approved the growth plan in principle, but, you want us to actually spend money on it?")

First one with the answers truly will be on to the Next Big Thing.

For Further Reading

Customer Centered Growth by Richard Whiteley and Diane Hessan (1996, Addison-Wesley)

Go for Growth! by Robert Tomasko (1996, John Wiley & Sons)

Grow to Be Great by Dwight Gertz and João P. A. Baptista (1995, Free Press)

Reprint U9606B

Strategies for Surmounting Special Challenges

• • •

Your unit or company may face numerous challenges that require savvy strategies. The articles in this section explore three such challenges and provide suggestions for crafting strategies that will help you overcome each. In the selections that follow, you'll discover how to help your company profit even during an economic downturn; how to run your division, department, or team even when you're understaffed; and how to ensure that your organization gains competitive advantage from outsourcing.

Taking Advantage of a Downturn

• • •

Sarabjit Singh Baveja, Steve Ellis,
and Darrell K. Rigby

Recessions are famous for breaking companies. But what few people realize is that recessions are in fact more likely to make a company's reputation.

A recent study by Bain & Company found that twice as many companies made the leap from laggards to leaders during the last recession as during surrounding periods of economic calm.

Case in point: Walgreens, the drugstore chain. In the midst of this last recession, the company focused on expanding its lower-cost, generic drug business. Earnings and sales for the fourth quarter of 2001 grew by

10.7% compared with the same period in 2000. Not only has Walgreens gained market share on its key competitors, but at a time when many drug retailers face capital constraints and a shortage of pharmacists, it plans to build 475 new stores and two new distribution centers this year.

Walgreens' success is not unique. The Bain study, which analyzed more than 700 firms over a six-year period that included the recession of 1990–1991, offers insight into how companies can take advantage of downturns. But first, you have to understand the strategic impact of a recession.

Recessions "shuffle the deck" more than boom times do.

The Bain study found more than a fifth of companies in the bottom quartile in their industries jumped to the top quartile during the last recession. Meanwhile, more than a fifth of all "leadership companies"—those in the top quartile of financial performance in their industry— fell to the bottom quartile. Only half as many companies made such dramatic gains or losses before or after the recession.

Arrow Electronics offers a striking example of trading places when times are tough. During an industry downturn in the late 1980s, the financially troubled distributor of electronic components and computer products launched a series of audacious but smart acquisitions that allowed it to increase sales by more than 500%, turn operating losses into profits, and seize market leadership from competitor Avnet, which was once twice Arrow's size. During the recent recession, Arrow has been acquiring again and widening its industry lead.

Gains or losses show up early.

Many managers tolerate subpar results during a recession, believing that their firms will accelerate past competitors once the economy recovers. This rarely happens. More than two-thirds of the companies that made major gains in our study period did so during a recession, not before or after.

In 2001, Dell Computer grew unit sales by 11% even as industry sales declined 12%. Realizing that price elasticity sometimes increases during a recession, Dell used sensible price cuts to gain more than six points in U.S. market share and, in the toughest period of all—the fourth quarter of 2001—to capture more than 90% of the profits in its industry.

Such opportunities always exist for strong companies, but the impact of exercising them is much higher during a recession, when many competitors are either distracted or hibernating.

Gains or losses made during recessions tend to endure.

Of the firms that made major gains in revenue or profitability during the last recession, more than 70% sustained those gains through the next boom cycle. The corollary was also true: fewer than 30% of those that lost ground were able to regain their positions. After losing significant ground during the retail downturns of 1987 and 1991, Kmart continued to slide downhill from there—all the way to a Chapter 11 bankruptcy in 2002. Meanwhile, Wal-Mart continued to invest in service infrastructure during these periods; rolling back prices, it gained an estimated 2% to 4% in comparable-store sales over Kmart and Target.

These findings show that recessions are not so much "slowdowns" as they are intense crucibles of opportunity. Why is this so? Good times can cushion the hard truths of company performance, whereas tough times reveal true strengths and weaknesses. Then, too, the number of strategic opportunities to make deals or to take advantage of weaker players increases during a recession. Many companies either hunker down or stray outside their core business in a desperate bid for growth, creating openings for companies willing to pursue thoughtful and balanced recession strategies. Judging from the experiences of the best performers of the last recession, the key is to stay focused.

Know Your Starting Point

The biggest failures from the last recession were companies that misunderstood their starting point and invested inappropriately. Example: Borden Milk Products, which diversified from its core in dairy products and lost market leadership. Winning firms undertake careful internal and external diagnostic inquiries at the beginning of a downturn. Identifying their key strengths and weaknesses, they develop a watertight definition of their core business and strategy. This provides a reliable yardstick by which to measure new strategic options.

Maintain Strategic Discipline

If the data says your core business is weak, don't try to invest through the downturn until you've fixed the problem. During the last recession, Mattel maintained a clear picture of its business needs. It reduced capacity, eliminated costs, and refocused manufacturing and management resources on its core brands: Barbie and Hot Wheels. It also forged a strategic alliance with Disney. By tending to its core, Mattel was able to grow despite the turbulence; in fact, it achieved double-digit annual growth in sales and income during the boom that followed.

In the late '90s, Mattel seemed to forget the importance of strategic discipline with its ill-advised acquisition of The Learning Company. But since divesting itself of The Learning Company, Mattel has gone "back to Barbie."

Correct Your Wrong Turns Promptly

Companies that fared poorly during the last recession exhibited a common response: they overreacted, then "stayed the course" even when rougher seas lay ahead. The lesson? If your strategy isn't showing results, reevaluate it. Don't expect it to start paying dividends just because the economy is recovering. Winning firms react to trouble early, scrapping ideas that aren't working and turbocharging those that are. Firms that hunker down can miss opportunities and create even bigger problems down the road.

In the recession of the late '80s, Kmart diversified to hedge its bet on a struggling core discount retail business. But the acquisition of a slew of unrelated retail businesses sapped much-needed resources and attention from Kmart's core. As the company struggled to manage and later unload these unrelated businesses, Wal-Mart and Target were able to make sizable inroads in many of Kmart's key markets and customer segments.

Even the deepest recessions have bright spots. Housing and some consumer goods segments, for instance, held up reasonably well in 2001. Conversely, boom times have dark spots: nearly 20% of U.S. industries will be battling downturns any given year. For companies hoping to get ahead during down times, the good news is that you may not have to wait long: your sector may experience some turbulence—well before the next recession.

Reprint U0209E

Strategies for the Shorthanded

• • •

Paul Michelman

Meet Cheryl Andrus: Manager. Survivor. A vice president responsible for corporate and product marketing at FranklinCovey, Andrus was asked in August 2002 to also take charge of one of the company's business lines. Along with these new responsibilities came the mandate to achieve 50% bottom-line improvement during the next year.

To do this, Andrus knew she would need a focused and dedicated team. What she had was an overburdened one. In fact, a company survey showed that 60% of Andrus's 48 reports believed that they were working at maximum capacity and couldn't take on any additional work. (The nationwide average in FranklinCovey's xQ survey was 50%.)

What's more, over the course of the next six months, the size of Andrus's already overtaxed staff would shrink from 48 to 35—but corporate expectations would not be ratcheted down.

Andrus had quite a challenge on her hands. Perhaps you are attempting to manage your way through a similarly exigent scenario. Trying to accomplish everything that used to be done by two or three people, you may be feeling stressed, maybe more than a bit underappreciated. But take heart: You can weather this storm and come out on top—if you have a strategy.

> Regular team meetings, along with plenty of one-on-ones, help ensure that short-term objectives support long-term goals.

A well thought out plan for managing yourself, your team, and even your boss through these tough times will not only help you address the new demands being heaped upon you, it will also help you turn this onerous situation into a springboard for future growth.

Let's begin with what you shouldn't do: "The sure recipe for failure is to suck it up and try to do it all," says Isabel Parlett of Parlance Training, a firm specializing in business communications. "You'll burn out, your team will resent you, your reputation will suffer, and the work probably won't all get done anyway."

Conversely, if you offer resistance to new duties when the company is down, you may not like the company's reaction. Even if you don't find yourself on the wrong end of a future workforce reduction, you'll likely be tagged with the dreaded "not a team player" label, and future opportunities could be severely limited.

So what's the recipe for successful self-management in this economic climate? The ingredients include balance, focus, effective communication, and more than a pinch of dynamism.

Those were certainly apparent in Andrus's response to her rather large dilemma. "I had a problem," she says, "but there were very specific things I focused on to help me through the dark days and deliver value to the company." Here are two facets of her approach.

Stay Focused

Since Andrus clearly could not accomplish everything on her agenda, she says she brought "very intense" focus to determining which of her many goals were truly critical—to her, her team, and the company. To do so, she applied a five-part litmus test to each of her existing goals by asking these questions:

- "WHAT IS ITS ECONOMIC IMPACT?" How will this goal affect the company economically and move it forward?

- "IS IT ALIGNED WITH THE COMPANY'S STRATEGY?" In a time of rapidly shifting corporate strategy, it's essential to regularly reevaluate individual and team goals to ensure that each still maps to those of the company.

- "HOW WILL IT SATISFY STAKEHOLDERS?" How important is it to your boss, your team, and other interested parties?

- "WHAT IS MY LEVEL OF PASSION, TALENT, AND ENERGY FOR IT?" If you can't bring all three to the table, you're not going to achieve a high return on your efforts.

- "DO WE HAVE THE RESOURCES?" Is there sufficient time, money, and any other necessary resources to accomplish this goal?

Ultimately, you can't determine which goals rate as must-do's entirely on your own, Andrus says. "After I go through this process myself, I go see my boss to make sure I'm aligned with him and with his stakeholders. You have to learn to be open and to listen to how your boss reacts to your analysis. By focusing on economic impact and strategy in particular, you are talking in his language, and it makes you look smart."

Many managers are daunted by the prospect of having these types of conversations with their bosses, notes Thomas DeLong, who teaches organizational behavior at Harvard Business School. "I'm amazed that although organizations are willing to set metrics for success in difficult times, so few individuals are willing to have conversations about what they need to accomplish," he says.

The toughest thing for most people is initiating this type of discussion, DeLong continues. In his work with professional service firms, he's found that many people would rather work 80 hours per week than hold difficult conversations about their workload.

> If your team has learned valuable lessons that could provide benefits to other areas in your supervisor's domain, offer to facilitate some cross-team learning.

So how do you broach this delicate subject? "When in doubt, share the dilemma," DeLong says.

For example, you might start a conversation with your boss like this: "I'm excited about the opportunities I have. But I have 10 great opportunities and the time for four. If you were me, how would you approach this?"

Remember the Little Picture

At a time when her team was filled with fear and feeling burnt out, Andrus used small successes as a motivational tool. First, make sure everyone understands the long-term strategy, she says. Then, "if you get people focused on current results, even small milestones and successes can get people energized really quickly."

Andrus practices what her company's products preach: She holds both regular team meetings and one-on-ones with her direct reports; she also underscores the importance of having daily and weekly priorities. It's all part of making sure that short-term objectives support long-term goals.

Andrus's strategy appears to be working well. She still has her sanity, and her team is moving ahead: "It's been a slow start, but we're making faster progress every month. So far it looks like we can make it [to the 50% improvement] by the end of the year."

Andrus's experiences and the strategy she employed dovetail nicely with the best advice we heard from a number of self-management experts. Here are their suggestions for overburdened managers.

Get Out in Front

"No one in the organization wants to be the one to decide what has to give" when there is a loss of staff, says Parlance Training's Parlett. "So everyone plays corporate hot potato, passing the problem down the line until someone ends up as the scapegoat for not pulling off a miracle. Stepping up to the plate and making the call about what gets done and what doesn't can make you the hero. You do the deed no one else wants to do, and you focus your efforts toward producing the results you've decided are most meaningful."

Create Alliances

"Senior managers should develop networks of internal alliances," says Larraine Segil, author of *Dynamic Leader, Adaptive Organization: Ten Essential Traits for Managers.* These are cross-group relationships that are strategically mapped to include stakeholders with direct relationships to managers' areas of influence. Such internal alliances not only augment your current efforts, they also help your work get noticed.

"Keeping your head down under the burden of responsibilities will mean that your personal and strategic vision will be stymied within your own organization," Segil notes. If you miss the opportunity to court key opinion influencers, they won't be able to assist you when you need help later.

DeLong urges executives to create support networks of "truth speakers." Within your organization, you should seek out two or three people "who will tell you the things you don't want to hear and who will give a fair representation of who you are when you're not in the room," he says. "The last thing we need when things are tough is to have people tell us what they think we want to hear."

Manage Up

"Remind your superiors about your added responsibilities," says Susan Battley, CEO of Battley Performance Consulting, and a leadership psychologist for many Fortune 100 firms. "Human nature being what it is, they are likely to forget or overlook this change if you don't." This can be tricky since you don't want to be seen as a whiny opportunist during difficult times. Seek regular feedback from your boss about your expanded duties, Battley recommends. "This can be a subtle and effective reminder," she says; it keeps your new duties in the forefront of your superior's often frazzled mind while ensuring that you are contributing in the most effective way possible.

Focus on Your New Duties

The easiest thing to do when you're saddled with new projects is to give them short shrift. In the name of survival, it is tempting to make sure you know enough to manage current processes and leave it at that. This approach misses a big opportunity, says Felicia Zimmerman, author of *Reinvent Your Work: How to Rejuvenate, Revamp, or Recreate Your Career* and principal of Zimmerman Communication.

If you take the time to really understand your team's responsibilities, you can bring a fresh perspective on how to make their work more strategically valuable. "Get the team focused on what could they do differently to provide better results with greater efficiency," says Zimmerman. By doing this, you deliver more value today and set yourself up to deliver more value tomorrow.

To Position Yourself, Begin with Your Team

When you are taking on substantial new responsibilities, it's tempting to fancy yourself an essential component of the company's survival—or at least its short-term success. However, Zimmerman cautions against attempting to take advantage of this situation until you have shown concrete results. And when you do make your move, be careful to cast your successes in the light of the team's performance.

"You should be talking informally to your boss regularly," says Zimmerman. "Over coffee, you mention how well the team is responding to the challenges and the results they are seeing, with the emphasis always on the team, not on you individually."

Use these conversations to set up next steps. For example, if your team has learned valuable lessons that could provide benefits to other areas in your supervisor's domain, offer to facilitate some cross-team learning. This kind of proactive approach delivers short-term value and shows your commitment to the organization.

What you take away from Andrus's story and how you apply the advice of the experts, only you can determine. But almost everyone should be able to pull at least a small lesson from this observation: "A lot of executives are sitting around waiting for the next shoe to drop," Zimmerman notes. "Worse, many have buried their heads in the sand like ostriches. When you do that, another part of your anatomy is uncovered."

Reprint U0306B

How to Think Strategically About Outsourcing

• • •

Martha Craumer

Outsourcing used to be viewed as little more than a ho-hum tactic for reducing the costs of back-room functions such as payroll and IT. It didn't have much pizzazz and was never confused with a breakthrough management idea. But things started to change in the early '90s, as companies began outsourcing more strategically significant functions such as manufacturing and logistics, and even product design and other innovation-related activities. All of a sudden, outsourcing had morphed into a critical management tool.

Then came the inevitable backlash. Outsourcing, so simple in theory, was turning out to be pretty tough to execute well. It wasn't living up to its promise—companies were outsourcing the wrong things for the wrong reasons and going about it the wrong way. Indeed, a study by Cap Gemini Ernst & Young showed that only 54% of companies are satisfied with outsourcing, down from more than 80% a decade ago.

Even so, now's not the time to give outsourcing the bum's rush. Its status as a strategic management tool remains secure, even if its evolution to this point has been far from smooth. But to get real strategic value from your third-party relationships, you often have to throw out much of what you thought you knew—for example, that shibboleth about always maintaining control of customer touchpoints. Some of the biggest success stories out there are turning this old saw on its head. UPS Supply Chain Solutions handles everything from order taking to delivery to customer service for its clients.

Outsourcing can free managers to focus on more strategic, higher-value activities, but only if they discipline themselves to use the freed-up time appropriately. Ed Frey, a vice president at Booz Allen Hamilton, says he's seen clients take the outsourcing approach and then fail to reap its benefits because they micromanaged their outsourcing partners. To get the most out of outsourcing, companies need to think "longer-term, about moves with enterprise-level outcomes like improved ROI or greater shareholder returns," explains Jane Linder, senior research fellow and associate director of Accenture's Institute for Strategic Change. "Usually this means outsourcing with a focus on external results—like repositioning yourself in the marketplace or changing your value proposition to customers in some key way, versus using outsourcing to save 5% on the cost of an internal administrative process."

The real play with outsourcing, in other words, is to use it as a tool to drive strategic value, transform businesses, and even fundamentally change industry dynamics. Here's how.

Take Costs Out, Put Value In

As outsourcing continues to move beyond back-room functions into more strategic areas of the business, the standard bidding process is losing favor: more and more companies are realizing that their best partner is the one that offers them the greatest value, not necessarily the lowest cost.

In the high-tech industry, original equipment manufacturers (OEMs) like Cisco, IBM, Nortel, Palm, and Compaq have outsourced manufacturing to specialists like Solectron and Celestica. These contract manufacturers have expanded their services to include shipping, repairs, and even product design. To this end, many are buying up engineering firms. By offering design services, the contract manufacturers hope to help craft products in a more standardized way to cuts costs and reduce the risk of component shortages, which can hurt a Cisco or a Compaq—especially when it has a hit product on its hands.

UPS Supply Chain Solutions adds value by acting as a consultant to its clients, often drawing on its expertise from one industry and applying it to another. Dan DiMaggio, the company's president, tells how UPS Supply Chain Solutions helped Fender Guitar rethink its decentralized, country-by-country distribution model in Europe: "We brought them what we considered to be some of the best practices in the high-tech industry." Now, instead of keeping stacks of inventory in each country, along with localized quality assurance and other value-added services, Fender uses a centralized, pan-European system that cuts inventory, warehousing, and transportation costs. UPS Supply Chain Solutions also provides value-added services like inspecting and tuning guitars in the warehouse, so that store owners get ready-to-sell products upon delivery. This adds speed and quality to the value equation—and gives Fender a competitive edge.

A Catalyst for Change

"Companies aren't very good at change," says Linder. "Whether it's changing their business model or implementing innovations or reengineering, it's hard work and people don't get everything they expect."

Some forward-thinking executives are beginning to use outsourcing as a change-management tool to drive major, enterprise-level transformation, such as a shift in competitive position or a major increase in market share or stock price. Transformational outsourcing can work because it goes outside for the critical missing piece, drawing on the expertise of a partner who can hit the ground running.

Linder cites the example of a troubled Spanish bank that offered only mortgages. Realizing that the company would go under if it didn't transform itself, the CEO converted the bank from a small mortgage operation into a full-service bank with a big data center and branches in all the major metropolitan areas of Spain—and in just a year's time. How? By outsourcing all information technology development and implementation. The bank contracted with third parties to manage the data center and product development, and used consultants to help open branches and hire and train staff. As a result, the bank was able to stem its losses, achieve breakeven operations, and attract a buyer.

Transformational outsourcing is often faster and more effective for organizations than other major change initiatives, such as reengineering or acquisitions. Explains Linder: "Companies have tended to use mergers and acquisitions to get themselves into new industries and change the boundaries of what they were doing. That's a very

What to Outsource: How to Tell Core, Noncore, and Strategic Activities Apart

In theory, outsourcing is a no-brainer. Companies can unload noncore activities, shed balance sheet assets, and boost their return on capital by using third-party service providers.

But in reality, things are more complicated. "It's really hard to figure out what's core and what's noncore today," says Jane Linder, senior research fellow and associate director of Accenture's Institute for Strategic Change. "When you take another look tomorrow, things may have changed. On September 9, airport security workers were noncore; on September 12, they were core to the federal government's ability to provide security to the nation. It happens every day in companies as well."

In some cases, companies leave themselves vulnerable to a market coup by former partners when they outsource. Such was the case with the German consumer electronics company Blaupunkt, notes Ed Frey, a vice president at Booz Allen Hamilton. To beef up the product line it offered to its dealers, Blaupunkt decided to add VCRs and contracted the work out to Panasonic (once a lowly circuit-board stuffer). Later, with the Blaupunkt reputation attached to its products, Panasonic approached the dealers directly and presto, it had a ready-made distribution network for its own product line. "In effect, all Blaupunkt did was give access to its dealer network to Panasonic," says Frey.

In their article "Linking Outsourcing to Business Strategy," authors Richard C. Insinga and Michael J. Werle advise companies to keep control of—or acquire—activities that are true competitive differentiators or have the potential to yield a competitive advantage, and to outsource the rest. They make a distinction between "core" and "strategic" activities. Core activities are key to the business but don't confer a competitive advantage, such as a bank's IT operations. Strategic activities are a key source of competitive advantage.

Because the competitive environment can change rapidly, the authors advise companies to monitor the situation constantly, and to adjust accordingly. As an example, they point to Coca-Cola, which decided to stay out of the bottling business in the early 1900s, partnering instead with independent bottlers and quickly building market share. The company reversed itself in the 1980s when bottling became a key competitive element in the industry.

blunt instrument—and hard to do right. With outsourcing, you get a finer point on your pencil."

Can Outsourcing Improve Industry Dynamics?

Frey believes that outsourcing has the potential to do away with the boom-and-bust cycles that many industries experience on an ongoing basis. Case in point: the recent high-tech meltdown—Frey contends that it was self-induced.

In times of strong or growing demand, he explains, OEMs like Cisco and IBM add cushions to the capacity forecasts they give to their contract manufacturers—think of it as a form of surge protection. For the same reason, their manufacturers add cushions to their own forecasts for needed components, so they don't get caught short. The result is speculative ordering on both ends of the value chain. This cushioning is completely independent of true demand; it wouldn't exist in a vertically integrated model, where manufacturing is done in-house and changing a forecast can be as simple as walking down the hall.

Outsourcing adds an extra layer to the supply chain, and that typically means one more safety cushion. These cushions didn't create the industry recession in and of themselves, but they heightened its severity. That's not to say that outsourcing is a bad thing—far from it. A company like Cisco probably couldn't have grown as big as it did as fast as it did with a vertically integrated model. Outsourcing allowed the company to use everyone else's manufacturing capacity instead of having to build its own plants.

Nevertheless, the high-tech supply chain could be vastly improved, says Frey: "I really believe that where outsourcing works is where it gets at some major source of waste, and the easiest one to find is risk—or the things you do to manage risk." That's why there's so much potential outsourcing value in the high-tech supply chain.

The solution, says Frey, is the strategic management of four levers: forecast, capacity, product design, and the relationship between the different parts of the value chain (who controls what). By learning how to adjust these settings to minimize and manage the inherent risks, companies can avoid the wasteful safety cushions that so often result.

Take product design, for example. The risks around component availability could be sharply cut by standardizing low-value components. "Do we really need 10 or 15 different kinds of CD-drive motors?" asks Frey. If the industry agreed on a smaller number of standardized components, the risk related to parts shortages would shrink dramatically.

Getting more value out of the high-tech supply chain comes down to "pooling component risk, pooling capacity risk, and standardizing the non-value- or low-value-added components of any product that comes out," Frey continues. And outsourcing is an integral part of that process.

For Further Reading

"Third-Party Logistics Study: Results and Findings of the 2001 Sixth Annual Study" by C. John Langley, Jr., Ph.D.; Gary R. Allen; and Gene R. Tyndall (2001, Cap Gemini Ernst & Young)

"Linking Outsourcing to Business Strategy" by Richard C. Insinga and Michael J. Werle (*Academy of Management Executive*, November 2000)

Reprint U0205B

About the Contributors

Marie Gendron is a contributor to *Harvard Management Update*.

Loren Gary is a contributor to *Harvard Management Update*.

Kirsten D. Sandberg is executive editor at Harvard Business School Press and a contributor to *Harvard Management Update*.

Paul Michelman is executive editor of HBR Specialty Publications and a contributor to *Harvard Management Update*.

Peter Jacobs is a freelance business writer based in Wellesley, Massachusetts.

John Hagel III, a Silicon Valley-based management consultant, spent 16 years as a partner at McKinsey and has also been a senior executive at several technology companies. He is the author of *Out of the Box: Strategies for Achieving Profits Today and Growth Tomorrow Through Web Services* (HBS Press, 2002).

Theodore Kinni is a business writer based in Williamsburg, Virginia.

Adrian Mello is a freelance writer based in northern California who covers business management and technology adoption issues and is a former editor in chief of *Line56, Macworld,* and *Upside.*

Sarabjit Singh Baveja is a vice president in Bain Consulting's San Francisco office.

About the Contributors

Steve Ellis is managing director at Bain Consulting.

Darrell K. Rigby is director of Bain's Boston office and author of the study "Winning in Turbulence."

Martha Craumer is a business and marketing writer based in Cambridge, Massachusetts.

Harvard Business Review Paperback Series

The Harvard Business Review Paperback Series offers the best thinking on cutting-edge management ideas from the world's leading thinkers, researchers, and managers. Designed for leaders who believe in the power of ideas to change business, these books will be useful to managers at all levels of experience, but especially senior executives and general managers. In addition, this series is widely used in training and executive development programs.

These books are priced at US$19.95
Price subject to change.

Title	Product #
Harvard Business Review **Interviews with CEOs**	3294
Harvard Business Review on **Advances in Strategy**	8032
Harvard Business Review on **Appraising Employee Performance**	7685
Harvard Business Review on **Becoming a High Performance Manager**	1296
Harvard Business Review on **Brand Management**	1445
Harvard Business Review on **Breakthrough Leadership**	8059
Harvard Business Review on **Breakthrough Thinking**	181X
Harvard Business Review on **Building Personal and Organizational Resilience**	2721
Harvard Business Review on **Business and the Environment**	2336
Harvard Business Review on **The Business Value of IT**	9121
Harvard Business Review on **Change**	8842
Harvard Business Review on **Compensation**	701X
Harvard Business Review on **Corporate Ethics**	273X
Harvard Business Review on **Corporate Governance**	2379
Harvard Business Review on **Corporate Responsibility**	2748
Harvard Business Review on **Corporate Strategy**	1429
Harvard Business Review on **Crisis Management**	2352
Harvard Business Review on **Culture and Change**	8369
Harvard Business Review on **Customer Relationship Management**	6994
Harvard Business Review on **Decision Making**	5572

To order, call 1-800-668-6780, or go online at www.HBSPress.org

To order, call 1-800-668-6780, or go online at www.HBSPress.org

Harvard Business Essentials

In the fast-paced world of business today, everyone needs a personal resource—a place to go for advice, coaching, background information, or answers. The Harvard Business Essentials series fits the bill. Concise and straightforward, these books provide highly practical advice for readers at all levels of experience. Whether you are a new manager interested in expanding your skills or an experienced executive looking to stay on top, these solution-oriented books give you the reliable tips and tools you need to improve your performance and get the job done. Harvard Business Essentials titles will quickly become your constant companions and trusted guides.

These books are priced at US$19.95, except as noted.
Price subject to change.

Title	Product #
Harvard Business Essentials: **Negotiation**	1113
Harvard Business Essentials: **Managing Creativity and Innovation**	1121
Harvard Business Essentials: **Managing Change and Transition**	8741
Harvard Business Essentials: **Hiring and Keeping the Best People**	875X
Harvard Business Essentials: **Finance for Managers**	8768
Harvard Business Essentials: **Business Communication**	113X
Harvard Business Essentials: **Manager's Toolkit ($24.95)**	2896
Harvard Business Essentials: **Managing Projects Large and Small**	3213
Harvard Business Essentials: **Creating Teams with an Edge**	290X
Harvard Business Essentials: **Entrepreneur's Toolkit**	4368
Harvard Business Essentials: **Coaching and Mentoring**	435X
Harvard Business Essentials: **Crisis Management**	4376
Harvard Business Essentials: **Time Management**	6336
Harvard Business Essentials: **Power, Influence, and Persuasion**	631X
Harvard Business Essentials: **Strategy**	6328
Harvard Business Essentials: **Decision Making**	7618
Harvard Business Essentials: **Marketer's Toolkit**	7626
Harvard Business Essentials: **Performance Management**	9428

The Results-Driven Manager

The Results-Driven Manager series collects timely articles from *Harvard Management Update* and *Harvard Management Communication Letter* to help senior to middle managers sharpen their skills, increase their effectiveness, and gain a competitive edge. Presented in a concise, accessible format to save managers valuable time, these books offer authoritative insights and techniques for improving job performance and achieving immediate results.

These books are priced at US$14.95
Price subject to change.

Management Dilemmas:
Case Studies from the Pages of
Harvard Business Review

When facing a difficult management challenge, wouldn't it be great if you could turn to a panel of experts to help guide you to the right decision? Now you can, with books from the Management Dilemmas series. Drawn from the pages of Harvard Business Review, each insightful guide poses a range of familiar and perplexing business situations and shares the wisdom of a small group of leading experts on how each of them would resolve the problem. Engagingly written, these interactive, solutions-oriented collections allow readers to match wits with the experts. They are designed to help managers hone their instincts and problem-solving skills to make sound judgment calls on everyday management dilemmas.

These books are priced at US$19.95
Price subject to change.

Title	Product #
Management Dilemmas: **When Change Comes Undone**	5038
Management Dilemmas: **When Good People Behave Badly**	5046
Management Dilemmas: **When Marketing Becomes a Minefield**	290X
Management Dilemmas: **When People Are the Problem**	7138
Management Dilemmas: **When Your Strategy Stalls**	712X

How to Order

Harvard Business School Press publications are available worldwide from your local bookseller or online retailer.
You can also call

1-800-668-6780

Our product consultants are available to help you
8:00 a.m.–6:00 p.m., Monday–Friday, Eastern Time.
Outside the U.S. and Canada, call: 617-783-7450
Please call about special discounts for quantities greater than ten.

You can order online at

www.HBSPress.org